America in Contemporary Soviet Literature

America in Contemporary
Soviet Literature

Alayne P. Reilly

New York   New York University Press
London   University of London Press Ltd
                                          1971

Acknowledgments

Selection from "The Lesson for Today" from THE POETRY OF ROBERT FROST edited by Edward Connery Lathem. Copyright 1942 by Robert Frost. Copyright © 1969 by Holt, Rinehart and Winston, Inc. Copyright © 1970 by Leslie Frost Ballantine. Reprinted by permission of Holt, Rinehart and Winston, Inc.

Quotations from the poetry of Mayakovsky reprinted here by permission of The World Publishing Company from THE BEDBUG AND SELECTED POETRY by Vladimir Mayakovsky, translated by George Reavey and Max Hayward. Copyright © 1960 by The World Publishing Company.

Excerpts from the poetry of Yevtushenko, translated by John Updike and Albert C. Todd from *Holiday* November 1968. Reprinted by special permission of Holiday, copyright © 1968 by The Saturday Evening Post Company.

"OZA" by Andrei Voznesensky from THE NEW RUSSIAN POETS 1953-1966 Selected, Edited and Translated by George Reavey. Copyright © 1966 by George Reavey. Reprinted by permission of October House Inc.

Preface

This book was undertaken because of the writer's deep interest in Soviet-American relations and the noticeable trend during the 1960's toward honest, non-propagandist descriptions of America by several leading Soviet writers. The findings of the study are far more revealing and extensive than had been supposed, and should be of interest to the general reader as well as to the specialist in Soviet affairs.

All of the sources are readily available outside the Soviet Union; indeed, several have been published only in the West. English translations of most of the works can be found in any university library.

Unless otherwise specified all translations from the Russian are my own. As for the transliteration of Russian words found in the text and the notes, scholarship defers to readability and accepted usage. However, standard transliteration is followed in the Bibliography.

I wish to express my deepest appreciation to the late Professor Robert Magidoff, and to Professor Leonid

Rzhevsky, both of New York University. Their patience, guidance, and encouragement made this undertaking possible, and it is with gratitude that I dedicate this work to these two distinguished gentlemen.

Alayne P. Reilly

Contents

PREFACE V

INTRODUCTION ix

PART I The Genesis of Propagandist Caricature

1 Four Early Impressions: Gorky, Mayakovsky,
Pilnyak, Ilf and Petrov 3

PART II The Emergence of a More Positive Image

2 Discovery: Andrei Voznesensky, Poems 49

3 Observation: Victor Nekrasov, *On Both Sides of
the Ocean* 79

4 Confrontation: Valentin Kataev, *The Sacred
Well* 117

5 Allegory: Yevgeny Yevtushenko, Poems 173

CONCLUSION 205

A SELECTED BIBLIOGRAPHY 209

INDEX 215

vii

Introduction

The metamorphosis of the image of America in recent works of several Soviet writers has been so vivid and meaningful that it becomes a rewarding subject for literary investigation. This study examines the evidence of a new attitude as found in the works of four poets and writers who have visited America during the past decade. Their impressions reflect a significant pause in the ideological warfare that has characterized the Soviet arts for decades and cramped the literary expression of her artists.

America has long held an especial fascination for the Russian people. Through the writings of American authors from Benjamin Franklin to Fenimore Cooper and Mark Twain, Russians have become acquainted with the democratic ideals of the American Revolution as well as with life in the United States in all its diversity. Prior to the Russian Revolution this literary acquaintance had fostered a widespread conception of the country "as a man-made paradise, and of Americans as muscular, upright, free and happy demigods." [1] This attitude toward

America will be seen in the initial reaction of Maxim Gorky to New York City and its people—although the same Maxim Gorky would later initiate the intensely negative caricature portrayal of America that was to be adopted by the Soviets once they had consolidated their power.

By 1932 Stalin had secured complete control over the arts with the formation of a single Party-regimented Union of Soviet Writers. Socialist realism was proclaimed the only acceptable literary doctrine; it demanded that the writer portray Soviet socialism in its idealized state, and the enemy, Western capitalism, as negatively as possible. America, as the leading capitalist country, became the prime target of a propaganda war directed at the annihilation of all ideological enemies.[2]

After the end of World War II, the propaganda campaign was intensified: "The thesis that the world is divided into two camps, one representing the rising forces of socialism and the other the decaying but aggressive forces of capitalism, has permeated all phases of Soviet propaganda and policy, both domestic and foreign, since the summer of 1947." [3] This policy continued unrelentingly until the death of Stalin in 1953. The liberalizing trends that followed his death, a period generally referred to as the "Thaw," lost considerable momentum in early 1963, when then Premier Khrushchev declared war on the burgeoning concept of peaceful coexistence. In a speech on March 8th at a meeting of Party officials with the Artists' Union he said in part:

> We adhere to class positions in art that are resolutely opposed to the peaceful coexistence of socialist and bourgeois ideologies. Art belongs to the sphere of ideology. Those who think that in Soviet art there

can be peaceful cohabitation of socialist realism and
formalist, abstractionist tendencies will inevitably slip
into the position of peaceful coexistence in the sphere
of ideology, a position that is alien to us. We have
recently encountered such ideas. Unfortunately, this
bait has been taken by some Communist writers
and artists, and even some officials of creative
organizations.[4]

This outburst was prompted in part by the American
travel memoirs of Victor Nekrasov and the American
poems of Andrei Voznesensky, which presented an image
of the United States that differed significantly from the
caricature image of their predecessors. Khrushchev was removed from his post a few months later and the rebellion
against propaganda continued among liberal writers. In
1966 Valentin Kataev, an old socialist-realist master, suddenly broke from his forty-year-long conformity to Party
literary doctrines and published an unorthodox surrealistic work that was in part about his trip to America. In
1967 the poet Yevgeny Yevtushenko began to publish a
series of poems about America that contained allegorical
allusions to the Soviet Union.

As will be shown, a new art form clearly seems to be
emerging among some of the more talented contemporary
Soviet writers, a form of personal expression that runs directly counter to the tenets of socialist realism. This feature was first noticed in writers like Mikhail Bulgakov
(1891–1940), who resorted to what Leonid Rzhevsky has
called *tajnopis'* [cryptography] to try to communicate
thoughts, criticisms, and philosophical reflections that
cannot be voiced openly.[5] To escape the censor's attention, the *tajnopis'* must be dispersed and concealed within
a deep camouflage. Bulgakov's surrealistic grotesque, how-

ever, failed to mislead the censor, who excised almost 15 percent of the text of *The Master and Margarita*.[6]

The writers of the sixties have been seeking new ways of camouflaging their ideas in a surrealism more oblique, and with protective devices more dependable, than Bulgakov's Gogolesque excursions into Russian life. Some of these writers have escaped into the genre of travel notes where the foreign environment offers a partial disguise for their thoughts. America especially has provided a convenient mask. Whereas previous works by Russian writers about the country had been straightforward descriptions of life in the United States, whether caricature, exposé, or objective reporting, the 1960's have seen the image of America being somewhat manipulated to serve as a background on which themes that relate to life in the Soviet Union are superimposed in clever and subtle ways. In some instances we have what amounts to a double exposure: the clear possibility of two different interpretations of a passage. In other instances the intentional ambiguity of the works tends to leave them beyond any clear deciphering.

Several of these creative works about America are analyzed in this study to determine what changes in form and style have evolved to camouflage the change in attitude and content. The study is limited to those writers and poets (as opposed to journalists) who have actually visited America and who have written travel memoirs or creative works based on the impressions from their trips. To permit a thorough analysis, the discussion is confined to the works of four important Soviet writers whose published impressions offer evidence of a significant revolution in the Soviet image of America: Andrei Voznesensky, Victor Nekrasov, Valentin Kataev, and Yevgeny Yevtushenko. The first chapter discusses the formative phase of the propagandist image of America, from which these later works so strikingly depart, in the works of five early Soviet writers: Maxim Gorky, Vladimir Mayakovsky, Boris Pilnyak, and Ilf and Petrov, all of whom visited America and whose writings on their trips helped to mold a negative image of the United States as an unhappy land of exploitation and suffering. An attempt is also made to compare the stylistic devices of propaganda with those of creative literature. A writer's sincerity, personal thought, and creative artistry are reflected in the consistency of his style and the freshness of his imagery. It is significant to note that the more creative and imaginative the style of the writers examined in this study, the more objective and positive the image of America that emerges.

Notes

1. Robert Magidoff, "American Literature in Russia," *Saturday Review*, November 2, 1946, 45.
2. A policy approved by Gorky in his pamphlet entitled, "If the enemy does not surrender, annihilate him," [*Esli vrag ne sdaetsja, ego uničtožajut*] first published in *Pravda*, November 15, 1930.
3. Frederick C. Barghoorn, *Politics in the U.S.S.R.* (Boston 1966), 103–104.
4. *Pravda*, March 10, 1963.
5. Leonid D. Rzhevsky, *"Pilatov grex: tajnopis' v romane M. Bulgakova, 'Master i Margarita,'"* *Novyj žurnal*, No. 90 (March 1968). Reprinted in L. Rzhevsky, *Pročten'e tvorčeskogo slova*, New York University Press, 1970.
6. *Ibid.*

Part I
The Genesis of Propagandist Caricature

1.

Four Early Impressions: Gorky, Mayakovsky, Pilnyak, Ilf and Petrov

> There was another book on the night table—
> American Tales by progressive writers. Khorobrov
> could not verify these stories by comparing them
> with life, but the selection was astonishing. Every
> story contained some obligatory abomination
> about America. Venomously assembled, they made
> up such a nightmarish picture that one could only
> be amazed that the Americans had not yet fled
> the country or hanged themselves.[1]

This brief quotation from Alexander Solzhenitsyn's novel *The First Circle* deftly summarizes the Soviet literary treatment of America over the past half century. The early Soviet regime especially encouraged such unfavorable descriptions of America and sent several of its leading writers to the United State for firsthand glimpses of the capitalist country they were expected to discredit in their writings. Five writers played a major role in molding the Soviet negative image of America: Maxim Gorky, Vladimir Mayakovsky, Boris Pilnyak, Ilya Ilf, and Evgeny Petrov. All but Pilnyak were proud Bolsheviks and Communists. Gorky's contribution, ironically, may have been an accident of fate. His inability to raise capital

3

in America for the then struggling Bolshevik cause may have put the young revolutionary in a mood for vengeance. However, the other works were a priori ideological commitments. Except in some of Ilf and Petrov's writings on America, very little objectivity is to be found in these damning reports. We will examine them briefly before proceeding to the main interest of this study, the changing Soviet literary image of America in the 1960's.

Maxim Gorky: "The City of the Yellow Devil"

Maxim Gorky, regarded by most Soviet critics as the Father of Soviet Literature, may also be considered in some respects the progenitor of the Soviet literary attitude toward America. "The City of the Yellow Devil," [2] though written more than a decade before the October Revolution that brought the Soviets to power, has become to a large extent a prototype, in style and content, of the Soviet literary image of America. Indeed, the descriptive notes to this work characterize it as a portrayal of the "inhuman essence of the 'American way of life' which is devoid of compassion and spiritual beauty."

Gorky visited America in the spring and summer of 1906 to secure goodwill and financial support for the Bolshevik Party which was then smarting from its aborted 1905 revolution attempt. Gorky's initial expectations of America were positive. His works had been favorably received in America where there was a great deal of sympathy for the young revolutionary movement in Russia. When he first arrived, his mood was a happy one, as newspapers of the time report:

"It is not the great things of your city that appeal so much as your people. I can understand the great buildings towering into the air, the beauties of New York as I see them from my window and the marvelous development of commerce, industry and finance as it is explained to me, but it is the people themselves who rouse strange thoughts in me. In their attitude is something of the spirit of America. They stand erect; their faces are bright and clear and free from the cringing, cowering looks of people who have bowed beneath the lash through many generations.

. . . . .

"In a few days I hope to see your great buildings, your massive structures that have made New York famous. I will find it easy to understand them. I have seen in the faces and in the bearing of the people the spirit of America, and I can realize how easy it is for them to accomplish great things."[3]

"Look what a country this is! Free, beautiful and happy! Someday, perhaps, Russia will be blessed by the same happiness."[4]

The happy mood was brief. The next day the newspaper headlines carried scandalous reports that Gorky's traveling companion was not his wife, but an actress, Maria Andreeva, with whom he had been living for several years. They were evicted from their hotel and refused lodgings elsewhere. Gorky was understandably upset by the scandal. Though not legally divorced from his first wife because of the difficulties of obtaining a divorce in Czarist Russia, he had parted with her on amicable terms. Andreeva, a highly respected artist with the Moscow Art Theatre where Gorky's plays were performed, was accepted everywhere in Russia and in Europe as Madame Gorky. The scandal in New York was partly the unfortunate result of newspaper rivalries and of ploys by the Imperial Russian Embassy who wanted to discredit Gorky in America.[5] However, Gorky's outspoken support of the striking Idaho mine workers and the radical labor leaders Moyer and Haywood, then on trial for murder, compounded the furor. All social events in Gorky's honor were canceled, including a testimonial dinner at which Mark Twain was to have presided.

Gorky was deeply hurt by the turn of events and wrote an embittered caricature of his inhospitable host, New York. The extent to which his personal feelings may have influenced the writing of "The City of the Yellow Devil" can be seen by referring to the original version of this work, "The City of Mammon," published in *Appleton's Magazine* (New York: August 1905). This is a first-person description of Gorky's impressions of New York, part of which he later rewrote in its present form. Approximately one fifth of this first version is devoted to moralizing on American "moralists."

"The City of the Yellow Devil" portrays a New York that hardly seems in keeping with Gorky's earlier impressions of the city:

> This is a city. This is New York. On the shore stand twenty-story houses, silent and dark "skyscrapers." Square, lacking any desire to be beautiful, the dull, heavy buildings rise upwards, gloomy and boring. One feels an arrogant conceit in the very height and ugliness of each house. There are no flowers in the windows, and no children are to be seen.
>
> From afar the city resembles an enormous jaw

with uneven black teeth. It breathes clouds of smoke into the sky, wheezing like a glutton suffering from obesity.

Entering the city you feel you have fallen into a stomach of stone and iron, a stomach that has swallowed several million people, grinding and digesting them.

The streets resemble a slippery, greedy throat through the depths of which flow dark pieces of food for the city—living people. All around you—over your head, under your feet and alongside you—iron lives and roars, celebrating its victory. Awakened to life and animated by the power of Gold, it surrounds man with its spiderweb, strangling him, sucking his blood and brains, devouring his muscles and nerves, growing and growing, supporting itself on the silent stone and spreading the links of its chain wider and wider.[6]

The light and happy mood of Gorky's earlier comments has given way to a dark and depressing one in "Yellow Devil." The spirit of freedom and peace has changed to an atmosphere of oppression and terror. The "great buildings towering into the air, the beauties of New York" are now "dull, heavy buildings lacking any desire to be beautiful." The "marvelous development of commerce, industry and finance" has become a monstrous spider strangling the inhabitants of the city in its web. The "erect people with bright, clear faces" have become faceless zombies, "dark bits of food" for the monster city.

Gorky's "peristaltic" image of a monstrous digestive tract is illustrative of the caricature technique found in many Soviet writings on America. The mood is one of oppression; the style is naturalistically, often grotesquely, hyperbolic. Other main devices are the repetition of negatively painted pictures and the vulgarization of purportedly positive ones. Stylistically, the technique is easily seen to derive from a formula for propagandist, as opposed to creative, literature. In the passage cited above, a city grotesquely devours its citizens with a repetition that admits minimal narrational variation. The city itself is a "jaw," a "glutton," a "stomach," a "throat," and a spider. It "swallows up," "grinds and digests," "strangles," "sucks blood and brains" and "devours muscles and nerves." The last two rather vivid expressions seem to have pleased the author as he uses them a second time in the text. On page 20 and again on page 26, the walls of the city are described as "sucking up people." And in case the reader should miss the point, he is reminded four separate times that the inhabitants are "food" for the city.

This Pavlovian repetition of pet words and phrases is found in Gorky's description of the elements of the city as well. The word "filth" appears, both as noun and as adjective, no less than twenty-two times. "Dust," "smoke," "darkness," and "fog" reappear constantly. A full palette of adjectives rounds out his grim perspective: "dark," "heavy," "black," "grey," "gloomy," "somber," "dead," "stifling," "tedious," "rotten," "festering."

On the third day of his visit to New York, Gorky was taken for a ride through Central Park. A reporter describes his reaction:

> "Peace, peace; peace everywhere about me," he said as he passed the pond where a group of youngsters were sailing miniature international cup races. "There is peace in the faces of the children. There is the very spirit of peace in the sight of squirrels and

birds and free men among the trees in a great city like this. There is here no sign of the military oppression that stamps the cringing, cowering look of the coward upon the faces of strong men. These men are strong and upright and powerful in their freedom. They dare speak what they think and think what they please. It is a new world to me." [7]

In the pages of "Yellow Devil," however, the free spirit of America that so overwhelmed Gorky during his first few days in New York is somewhat differently portrayed: "Inner freedom—freedom of the soul, does not shine in the eyes of the people." [8] Life in America has become "life without sunlight, without song or happiness, in captivity to hard labor." Instead of finding "peace in faces of the children" playing in Central Park, he sees only a despairing caricature:

> The children are like flowers thrown out of the windows of the houses into the filth of the streets by some coarse hand. Nourishing their bodies on the greasy fumes of the city, they are pale and yellow, their blood is poisoned, their nerves are irritated by the ominous shriek of rusty metal, by the gloomy wail of enslaved lightening.
> Can these children possibly grow up into healthy, courageous and proud people?—one asks oneself. [9]

Gorky's naturalistic hyperbole is here characterized by an especial lack of aesthetic proportion or balance, effected by his copious, redundant, and synesthetic epithets. The city exudes *"greasy* fumes." The children are not only "pale" but "yellow"; their nerves are irritated not merely by the noise of metal, but by the *"ominous* shriek of *rusty* metal" as well as the "*gloomy* wail of *enslaved* lightning." Such excesses are typical of this work and serve to erode its artistic form and to render it somewhat ridiculous. The emotional extremes of Gorky's prose here are typical of the poetics of his early romantic period (note the rhetoric of his newspaper comments on the city as well) but such a concentration of extravagant exaggeration is unique to this work.

These brief selections are typical of "Yellow Devil" and are illustrative of what later was to become the preferred style of anti-American propaganda in Soviet literature: redundancy and extremes of hyperbole in a naturalistic vulgarization of the imagery concerning America.

Another part of the vulgarization technique is the simplistic reduction of people to stereotypes of "exploiter" and "exploited." The antagonist in this work is the "force of gold"; the protagonist is the "force of hunger." The city is described as enormous, overwhelming, oppressive: a "city-monster" [10]—and for variety, "monstrous city" on the following page. The oppressors are "ichthyosaurs of capital." [11] Man is portrayed, in contrast, as minuscule, overwhelmed, oppressed:

. . . man is an insignificant screw, an invisible dot amidst the ugly . . . [12]

. . . the little people disappear into this boiling mass like grains in a cup of broth, like chips in the sea. [13]

. . . never before have people seemed to me so insignificant, so oppressed. [14]

Lonely little people disappear like flies, falling into the darkness. [15]

The propagandist intent of "Yellow Devil"—which Gorky himself admitted had no artistic value [16]—can be seen from his continued positive descriptions of America in letters home during and after the writing of the work. On the first of May Gorky wrote Pyatnitsky.

America! Not everyone is fortunate enough to see it. It is interesting here, amazing, and deucedly pretty—which I had not expected. Three days ago we went for an automobile ride around New York. I tell you, such lovely, such overwhelming beauty on the shores of the Hudson! It is quite moving.[17]

In mid-May Gorky wrote Pyatnitsky to expect the manuscript of "Yellow Devil" through Berlin.[18] This would indicate that the work was written by early May. Yet toward the end of May he wrote to Amfiteatrov: "By God, this is a fantastic country for a man who is able and willing to work! [19]

The contradictory impressions of New York (the newspaper reports and Gorky's personal correspondence versus the text of "Yellow Devil") suggest that Gorky's motivation for writing this unfavorable portrait of New York may be partly due to his bitterness over the lack of success of his mission to America. On May 23 he wrote to Ladyzhnikov: "I did not count on such a swinish attitude toward myself when I came here, and I ask you to pass along to Russia, when you can, that such an attitude will interfere with my successful completion of the business that interests the Party.[20]

"Yellow Devil" is not a satire evincing intimate acquaintance; Gorky did not see much of America. He had not come as a tourist: "I shall not seek new subjects

for my pen in America, but shall write of conditions
as I know them in Russia." [21] He made quick visits to
Providence, Boston, and Philadelphia to speak to socialist
groups to raise money for the Bolshevik Party, and spent
most of his six months in America in the Adirondacks
writing his revolutionary novel, *Mother*.

Gorky's vivid caricature of America was to become
a model for the Soviet propagandist portrayal of capitalist
America. "The City of the Yellow Devil" remains a favor-
ite metaphor of contempt for New York to the present day.

Vladimir Mayakovsky:
Poems and Travel Notes

The Soviet poet Vladimir Mayakovsky was among
the first Russian writers to visit America after the 1917
Revolution. In the summer of 1925 he made a three-month
visit sponsored by the American communist press. Entering the United States from Mexico, he visited Laredo,
New York City, Chicago, Philadelphia, Detroit, Pitts-
burgh, and Cleveland. The trip produced a cycle of
poems, "Poems about America," and some travel notes,
"My Discovery of America." [22] Most of these recorded impressions are about New York. The introduction to these
poems and travel memoirs describes them as a portrait of
"the overseas capitalist power in the full armor of its
technological developments and in the full squalor of its
spiritual culture and its moral depravity."

This is a fairly accurate assessment of Mayakovsky's
image of America. Like Gorky, he concentrates on pro-

pagandist caricature. The "squalor of its spiritual culture" is shown in the portrayal of capitalist money mad-
ness. What Gorky described as the "force of gold," Mayakovsky portrays as dollar worship: "Dollar-God, dollar-
Son, dollar-Holy Ghost," he writes in his travel notes.[23]
· The hyperbole continues:

> The relationship between an American and the dollar
> is a poetical one. . . . The American has an aesthetic
> fondness for the green color of the dollar and identi-
> fies it with spring. . . . Upon meeting, an American
> does not greet you with an indifferent "Good Morn-
> ing." He sympathetically cries, "Make money?" and
> goes on.

The American people are characterized as a "union
of foreigners for exploitation, speculation, and trade." [24]
America's "moral depravity" is disclosed in Mayakovsky's
description of the commercial relationship between the
sexes:

> If an American takes a woman to dinner, he
> kisses her without delay and demands that she kiss
> him. Without this "little act of gratitude" he would
> consider the dollars spent on dinner wasted, and
> would never go anywhere with this ungrateful woman
> again. And the woman's sensible and calculating
> friends would laugh at her.[25]

Mayakovsky is quiet expressive in his poems about
the American preoccupation with dollars. The following
is a brief excerpt from his poem, "Broadway":

They interrupt
                chewing gum
only to ask
            "Make money?"
A mother
        gives her breast
                    to her baby.
The baby,
        his nose dripping,
gives suck
        as if it were not a breast
                        but a dollar.
He's occupied
            with serious
                    business.[26]

This passage provides another example of the hyperbolic naturalism found in propaganda portraits of America.
Even a nursing mother, normally a sacrosanct image, is
not spared. The poetic meter is destroyed by a crude
attempt to caricature the image of the child ("his nose
dripping") and the inclusion of capitalist clichés ("make
money" and "occupied with serious business"). The poem
"100%" [27] offers yet another example of this naturalism.
It describes the birth of a one-hundred-percent American:
"weight, nine pounds, eyes like nickels." The upbringing
of the American child is similarly portrayed:

Very simple
            the question of upbringing.
He crawls,
        dirties his paws.
He smashes his brow—
                all right!
                    his nose—
all right!

The words "simple" [*prost*], "question" [*vopros*] and
"nose" [*nos*] provide some rhyme in Russian, but the
poem has no consistent poetic meter, and is essentially
colloquial prose in simulated verse form. The use of the
Americanism "all right" [*ol rajt*], typical of Mayakovsky
in this cycle, is an apparent attempt to provide local
color. The poems abound with such adapted expressions
as "make money" [*mek monej*], "business" [*biznes*], "subway" [*sobvej*], "how do you do" [*gau du ju du*], "I love
you" [*aj lov ju*], "thank you" [*senk'ju*], and so forth, usually employed in a derisory context.

The staccato form of Mayakovsky's verse lends itself
very well to propagandist effects in providing additional
stress for each phrase and heightening the emotional impact of the imagery. It also helps to obscure the *non-
sequiturs* in the content.

Mayakovsky's antidollar theme is as much an expression of his personal disinterest in money of any
nationality as it is an attack on America. Another poem
from his American cycle, "A Challenge," [28] contains an
unmistakably personal statement:

> I throw to the swinish devils
> all the dollars
>   of all countries.
> I'd like to end my life
>   in the trousers
>   I started in,
> accumulating
>   nothing
>   through my life.

Although a disdain for material possessions recurs
throughout Mayakovsky's works,[29] he is inclined to vul-

garize the American's feelings about money. The above stanza shows a noticeable improvement in imagery, poetics, and depth of thought from his poem "100%" where the baby capitalist is chided by his father for lack of initiative: "John, you're a good-for-nothing. / You've not earned a cent, / yet you're walking!" The beginning of the poem presents the poet's impression of a typical American:

> Shares—
>   bonds—
>   dollars—
>   cents—
> Rushing around in the dark provinces.
> That's how I pictured him,
>   that's how he impressed
>   me—
> The hundred-percent American.

Another characteristic of these propagandist verses is their pharisaical tone. The beginning lines of "A Decent Citizen" [30] appeal to "truly cultured men" (i.e., Soviet Communists) to observe the immorality and depravity of New York:

> If your eye
>   sees no enemy,
> if NEP and TORG
>   have depleted your ire,
> if you've
>   forgotten how to hate—
> come
>   here
>   to New York.

The poem then goes on to describe the garbage-
laden streets where the children play, the prostitutes, the
poverty, and so forth while the rich, morally unconcerned
capitalists thank God for their bounty over cocktails:

> While the owner
> > in the Hotel Plaza
> over a drink
> > feels near to God.
> Throwing
> > his eyes heavenward:
> "Thank you
> > for good business!"

Mayakovsky did not try to hide his admiration for
the technological accomplishments of America, and describes the "armor of its technological developments" mentioned in the introduction:

> If you need an office, there's no need to worry
> yourself over its construction. Just call someone on
> the thirtieth floor:
> "Hello! Prepare a six-room office for tomorrow.
> Twelve typists. A sign saying: "Great Renowned
> Trade of Compressed Air for Submarines." Two
> boys in brown hussar uniforms with star-banded
> caps. And twelve thousand forms with the above
> mentioned name. Good-bye."
> Tomorrow you can enter your office, and your
> receptionists will triumphantly greet you: "How do
> you do, Mr. Mayakovsky." [31]

The poet was especially enraptured by the Brooklyn
Bridge and wrote what may be considered an ode to its

Asfal't—steklo.
Idu i zvenju.
Lesa i travinki—
sbrity.
Na sever
s juga
idut avenju,
na zapad s vostoka—
strity.
A meždu—
(kuda ix stroitel' zavez!)—
doma
nevozmoznoj dliny.
Odni doma
dlinoju do zvezd,
drugie—dlinoj do luny.
. . . . .
Xočeš' pod zemlju—
beri sobvej,
na nebo—beri elevejter.

(Asphalt—glass. / I walk and jingle. / Trees and grass are clipped. / To north from south flow avenues / to west from east streets. / And between (what carried the builder away!) / houses of impossible height. / Some are as high as the stars / others as high as the moon / . . . To go underground—take the subway / skyward—the elevator.)

The rhyme and meter are lost in English, but the preciseness of the imagery is not. Besides "Brooklyn Bridge," these lines offer the only truly poetic images among Mayakovsky's American poems, and stand out in marked contrast to the doggerel of his propagandist verses.

Thus, Mayakovsky's reactions are somewhat ambivalent. He was impressed by much of what he saw in America, but as a devoted Communist he elected to throw his poetic talent into propagandist caricature.[37] His ironically "bourgeois" stubborn pride is clearly expressed in the ending of the poem "Broadway":

I'm ecstatic
            over the city of New York.
But I will not
            tip my hat.
Soviets have
            their special pride:
we look down
            upon the bourgeois.

In another poem, "The Americans Will Be Surprised,"[38] written in 1929 but included with the American cycle, Mayakovsky describes the astonishment of the Americans over the Soviet people who fulfill five-year plans in four years. However, the final quatrain reveals a tinge of envy within the attack:

Bourgeois,
            marvel
                  at the Communist shore—
in work
            planes
                  and trains
we shall catch
                  and overtake
your quick-footed
                  famous America.

Such messianic proclamation of the utopian wonders of Communism, along with the self-righteous indignation over the supposed miseries of capitalism, is perhaps the basic feature of Soviet writing about America.

The outstanding features of Mayakovsky's nonlyric poetry as a whole are his bombastic, sloganistic proclamation of the Soviet Communist way of life and his relentless attacks against the "enemies" of Communism. While many of his foreign poems are full of comments about the coming Soviet utopia, none of them are so outspoken nor so full of derisive caricature as his poems about America. A group of poems about France, also written in 1925, contains none of the naturalistic expression of his American poems. Mayakovsky seems to have been very fond of Paris. His French poems recall the splendor of French history (the court of Louis XIV) and the richness of her arts in the 1920's (Verlaine, Cezanne) as well as the charm of the city. In a farewell poem to Paris he writes that if he were not a Russian, he would like to live and die in Paris.[39]

As in the case of Gorky, Mayakovsky's quarrel with America is ideological. Whereas Gorky focuses attention on the city as oppressor in "The City of the Yellow Devil," Mayakovsky concentrates on the supposed depravity of the people of America in his poems and notes. Physical hunger was Gorky's motif: two decades later, greed—the hunger for money—has become Mayakovsky's *bête noire*. The style of both exploits the propagandist devices of naturalistic hyperbole, stereotyped images, Pavlovian repetition, and *non-sequitur*.

Boris Pilnyak:
Okay, An American Novel

Boris Pilnyak, unlike Gorky and Mayakovsky, was neither a Bolshevik nor a political writer. In his diary he once wrote: "I am not a Communist, and therefore I do not concede that I should be a Communist or write in a Communist manner." [40] Pilnyak belonged to the camp of writers who placed aesthetic criteria above the utilitarian doctrine of art favored by the Bolsheviks, and who struggled to preserve the freedom and independence of the writer from political control. Stylistically, he was associated wtih a group of southern writers from Odessa known for their "ornamental" language of vivid imagery and rhythmic prose. Pilnyak's novel, *The Naked Year*, a highly expressionistic work about the agonies of the Russian Civil War, was published in 1921. The book's unheroic treatment of the Red Army, as well as its experimental language forms, came into sharp disfavor with the new Soviet regime. Later Pilnyak wrote two stories that were also poorly received by the Soviets: "The Unextinguished Moon" (1926) about the rumored murder of the war hero Commander Frunze at Stalin's orders, and "Mahogany" (1929) about the continued stagnation of provincial life in Russia after the revolution.

Pilnyak visited America in 1931 in an attempt to atone for his devious work by writing a firsthand exposé of the supposed evils of capitalist life. I. M. Gronsky, then Chairman of the Organization Committee of the Writer's Union, mentioned Pilnyak's mission in a speech before the Second Plenary Session of the Committee in February 1933:

Pilnyak, an old writer, got entangled with the Trot-
skyites under whose influence he wrote a disgusting
thing, "Mahogany." We chastised him. Writers turned
their backs on him. But we Bolsheviks decided to
try again—perhaps something could be done. So we
sent him to Central Asia, and received his "Tadzhikian Sketches." Then he went abroad, mainly to
America, and wrote as a result of that trip a work
in which he truthfully described the condition of
capitalist countries, mainly America. The work turned
out to be not a bad one at all.[41]

Pilnyak traveled across America for three months,
going by train from New York to California and returning by automobile to New York. *Okay, An American
Novel* is an account of life in America as he saw it during
his travels.[42] The work is not a novel, as the title might
imply, but a long, rambling, publicist travel memoir that
is unworthy of Pilnyak's talents as a writer. There is
almost no sign of his earlier ornamental and rhythmic
prose. The leitmotif technique that was so successful in
The Naked Year has degenerated into Stakhanovite bathos
in *Okay*. A few propagandist terms become heavy motifs,
mournfully repeated throughout the three hundred pages
of text: "flags," "philistine," "Nietzschean dollars," "American individualism," "advertising," and numerous "och's"
and "ach's." The Ford conveyer belt turns into a negative
metaphor for American life in general. The roads become
"conveyer belts" of the capitalist society moving me-
chanically through a standardized life:

Really, one cannot escape from the conveyer
belts of America's roads, and really, to travel along

the conveyor belts of the American roads is no less tiresome than to work on Ford's conveyor belts.[43]

Ford is the American god and savior.[44]

America! The genius of America! Ford! The genius of Ford! For this principle—the birth of machines on the conveyor belt—has been adapted everywhere now, even in restaurants and by many merchants.[45]

Man is not a human being but an addition to a conveyor belt.[46]

Like Gorky and Mayakovsky before him, Pilnyak describes the American obsession with money:

But "Unto Caesar . . ." Truisms often happen to be true, and the truism that the dollar, and only the dollar is master, sovereign, dream, and the delight of American morality is the truest of truisms.[47]

American patriotism appears only when there is talk about the dollar or—the American flag! [48]

Dear Nietzschean dollar![49]

Mister capitalism is the Nietzschean dollar.[50]

The master of America and her leader is the Nietzschean dollar.[51]

The prominent display of the American flag everywhere he went, "even in cemeteries," seems to have bothered Pilnyak. He sarcastically describes the "three whales" of American democracy as the Bible, the Constitution, and the national flag.[52]

New York is described as "inhuman," although he seems to have felt a twinge of admiration for the buildings of the city when viewed from above: "From the sixtieth, the hundredth floor, New York is striking, indescribable, extraordinary, ominous, an ominously beautiful city—a city of the triumph of industry, of the scope of human skill." [53] He continues his description of New York from below in somewhat different terms:

> But if you walk along the streets of New York, it is a terrible city, the most terrible city in the world, no matter whether you are on Park Avenue or on the Bowery. The city is deafened with noise. The city breathes gasoline instead of air. The city is victimized by the prostitute-like beauty of its electric advertisements. The streets are strewn with garbage, without a single leaf. . . . A city in which it is impossible for man to live.[54]

Pilnyak reports visiting a millionaire on the thirtieth-floor roof garden of his skyscraper and looking down on the roofs of smaller neighboring buildings:

> The sunset was beautiful, the roof of the neighboring building was littered with orange peels thrown there no doubt from the roof of my poor millionaire's home, since the legend of heavenly manna, like the legend of heavenly oranges, cannot be explained by the laws of physics. Oh, how sinister and inhuman

New York is from a skyscraper. Och, America! Ach, America of national flags that fly even over cemeteries! Ach, American Nietzschean individualism! [55]

One wonders how the laws of physics would explain orange peels falling straight down for twenty-five stories —they might be more inclined to hit the roof from the hands of tenants sunning thereon. The emotional illogicality of the scene is typical of propagandist writings. The capitalist is by nature guilty. The inhabitants of the smaller buildings are by nature not inclined to leave garbage behind when they go up on their roofs. Also typical is the introductory sentence about the sunset. Such scenes seem more effective when contrasted to the beauty of nature.

Pilnyak visited America in 1931 in the midst of the depression, a time when America may indeed have seemed on the brink of collapse. Although curiously enough he does not dwell on the depression at any length. He concentrates instead on the usual propaganda themes: poverty of the masses versus the wealth of depraved millionaires; exploitation and the inhumanity of capitalism; mistreatment of Negroes and Indians; gangsterism and crime. He seems preoccupied with conveyor belts, national flags, and Nietzschean dollars. He makes only a few attempts to herald the coming of Communism.

But Pilnyak's heart apparently was not in his task. *Okay* is weakly written, with no real consistency of theme or content. Poor Pilnyak was writing for his life and apparently hoped he could make up for his lack of inspiration by persistent repetition of key propagandist clichés. The mood throughout is laboriously negative. His imagination is not fired either by America or by his commissioned exposé. The closest he comes to his earlier ornamental style is in a brief description of the only things in America that he liked: the cactus desert in the West and Niagara Falls. In these passages he is obviously moved—his writing becomes fresh, imaginative, and almost lyrical, especially in comparison with the awkward style and expression of the rest of the book:

> The cactus desert lies below the Sierra Nevada mountains in the ghastly intense heat of the sun, in the yellow sand. It does not even vaguely resemble real nature, but sketches in the imagination a dead sea bottom where cacti—huge and terrible yuccas and wild palms—resemble sea plants and reefs of sea animals. The yucca does not have only one leaf-bearing cap but several: suddenly a cap resembling a crown protrudes from a bare and ragged trunk. The cacti are of diverse shapes. Some are yellow and prickly like porcupines; some are smooth and green like cucumbers. The small ones are about the size of a prairie dog; the huge ones are as big as three grown Indians. Both the palms and the cacti protrude from the sand that creeps beneath them as if they were casually and only temporarily stuck into the sand.[56]

> Niagara Falls—truly majestic, unique and powerful is this Colossus of water falling from the granite heights. It is indescribable, as are all things or events that are sublime in their simplicity. . . . Near it one must remain silent, near this mechanical (as opposed to volcanic, for example) manifestation of the might of nature, the colossal power of her geologic factory. Factories and plants built around it . . . are mere puppies beside this factory of water and granite.[57]

Unlike Mayakovsky who forgot nature after he saw electricity, Pilnyak remains awed only by the grandeur of nature. This may also account for some of his negative reactions to the big cities of America. Pilnyak's publicist novel was not well received in the Soviet Union despite Gronsky's initial favorable comment. For all the author's derogatory conveyor-belt remarks, a chapter on the statistics of American production and remarks on the possibility of buying a used car for 25 rubles,[58] among others, inadvertently proclaimed the vast superiority of American technology and the comparative comfort of her way of life, even during a depression. Pilnyak's efforts at rehabilitation did not succeed. After his trip to America, he visited Japan and wrote a book about that trip. But in 1937 he was arrested as a Japanese spy and vanished from among the living. His book on America, unlike the American writings of Gorky, Mayakovsky, and Ilf and Petrov, is never mentioned by Soviet critics and has not been republished. The 1934 Literary Encyclopedia characterizes *Okay* as follows:

> Pilynak gives a picture of the daily, national, and industrial relationships in America. He uncovers the depravity of capitalist technology (the Ford conveyor belt). Pilnyak rightfully declares that he wrote *Okay* to explain once more to our American brother workers the capitalist servitude of their existence. Written in the form of a publicist novel, the work is evidence that while having reformed himself ideologically, Pilnyak is still not able to represent reality in meaningful artistic imagery.[59]

Pilnyak's keen awareness of the world scene is reflected in a simple sentence in the beginning of *Okay*:

"Today the Soviet Union and the United States are playing chess with contemporary humanity." It is this theme more than any other that seems to concern many Soviet writers of today.

Ilf and Petrov:
One-Storied America

The well-known Soviet humorists, Ilya Ilf and Evgeny Petrov, offered the Russian reader a trifold image of America in three very different works that resulted from their trip to America in the midthirties: a fairly objective and comprehensive description of the land, its people, and its everyday life in their travel memoir, *One-Storied America;* [60] a tendentious short story about a young Soviet girl's experiences in capitalist America, "Tonya"; [61] and a humorous satirical sketch describing Columbus' impressions of twentieth-century America, "Columbus Moors to the Shore." [62] By far the most significant work, for the image of America it presents to the Soviet reading public, is the lengthy account of their travels in America, *One-Storied America.*

Ilf and Petrov visited America for four months in late 1935. Purchasing an automobile, they drove across America covering some ten thousand miles and visiting twenty-five states. They explored everything from stock car races, rodeos, and boxing matches to prisons, factories, and film studios. *One-Storied America* is an informal and intimate account of their trip which involves the reader in the details of their planning, their setbacks, and their adventures. The style is straight-forward and sober—there is almost no trace of the renowned satirical style of their earlier works. *One-Storied America* is a serious assignment for the pair. The authors come as devoted Communists to report firsthand on the life of a country whose capitalist way of life they consider alien to their own. But unlike their predecessors, they do not let their political leanings interfere with their craftsmanship as writers or with the honesty of their reporting. What they do not like in America is reported calmly and for the most part rationally. They do not harp repeatedly on the tiresome themes of propaganda.

Thus, *One-Storied America* marks the beginning of a three-dimensional image of America in Soviet writings. Ilf and Petrov unhesitatingly report the good along with the bad. The work also marks the discovery of rural America for the Russian reading public, heretofore acquainted mainly with the skyscrapers and slums of New York City. Now a whole new panorama lay before them: "America is basically a country of one and two-storied buildings. The great majority of the American population lives in small towns of three, five, ten or fifteen thousand people." [63] It is this America, the land of small towns, the "land of automobiles and electricity,"[64] that the authors describe for their reader:

> When we shut our eyes and try to resurrect in memory the country in which we spent four months, we do not see before us Washington with its gardens, columns, and assorted monuments, nor New York with its skyscrapers, its poverty and its wealth, nor San Francisco with its steep streets and suspension bridges, nor hills nor factories nor canyons, but a crossroads with a gasoline station set against a background of telegraph wires and advertising signs.[65]

Ilf and Petrov's guide to America is the middle-aged, good-natured, and absent-minded Mr. Adams.[66] He and his wife Becky, who serves as chauffeur for the group, are used by the authors as a device to weld the narrative as well as to provide comic relief with their petty squabbles over Mr. Adams' forgetfulness—he continually misplaces his hat and glasses, walks through a plate glass window, loses the car keys, neglects to return motel keys, and so forth. He also acts as a spokesman for American accomplishments, as a critic of American injustices, and as an admirer of the Soviet Union.

One-Storied America is divided into five parts covering different regions of the authors' travels: New York City; the Eastern states; across the nation to the Pacific Ocean; the West; and the relatively quick trip back to New York. The book is written from their carefully kept diary notes and follows the time and geographical sequence of their travels. The most important impressions of their trip are related.

The authors found car travel through America to be convenient and inexpensive. Their accommodations were always comfortable and clean: "We became so accustomed to good roads, good facilities, cleanliness, and comfort, that we stopped paying attention to them." [67] American food, however, is a major complaint: "Generally speaking, if one may speak of bad taste in food, then American cuisine undoubtedly appears as an expression of bad, absurd, and eccentric taste." [68]

American movies are another subject of major criticism. The authors went to the movies almost every night during the trip and saw over a hundred films.[69] They devote quite a few pages to a discussion of Hollywood. Although they admired the technological brilliance of the film industry, they deplored the content of its product:

"All of these films are below the level of human dignity. It seems to us that to watch such movies is a humiliating occupation for a human being." [70]

The contrast between poverty and plenty under the capitalist system, a frequent criticism of America, is also noted by Ilf and Petrov. They comment about it quite strongly, but do not dwell repeatedly upon it.

Even from the point of view of capitalism that has elevated the simultaneous coexistence of wealth and poverty to the status of law, Chicago must appear a dreary, clumsy, uncomfortable city. There is probably nowhere else on earth where heaven and hell are so intimately intertwined as in Chicago. Side by side with the marble and granite facing of skyscrapers on Michigan Avenue are disgusting sidestreets, filthy and stinking.[71]

Interestingly enough, they do not note any such contrasts in the smaller towns and cities they visit. The contrast between rich and poor, between skyscrapers and slums, seems to be their main objection to the big cities such as New York and Chicago. The Negro problem is mentioned only in passing. Ilf and Petrov also visited Indian reservations in New Mexico, and describe the Indians as poor but proud of their own heritage and refusing to participate in the white man's world. In general, there is little of the exploitation-caricature that is so prevalent in earlier and later Soviet works on America.

Ilf and Petrov are especially delighted by the natural beauty of America, and by her National Parks in particular. Some of their descriptive passages of the American landscape are quite lyrical, and their vivid imagery recalls the style of the ornamental school to which they, like Pilnyak, belong. Here they describe the painted desert:

> Smooth sandhills stretched to the horizon like a stormy ocean whose waves had suddenly turned to stone. They crept upon one another, forming crests and thick round folds. They were magnificent, brilliantly painted by nature in blue, pink, reddish-brown, and pale yellow. The tones were dazzlingly pure.
>
> The word "desert" is frequently used as a symbol of monotony. But the American desert is unusually varied. The appearance of the desert changes every two or three hours. We passed hills and cliffs that resembled pyramids, towers, recumbent elephants, and antediluvian pangolins.[72]

The authors make an interesting observation on the symphonic merging of the works of man with the works of nature:

> The region in which we drove was utterly wild and desolate, but we did not feel isolated from the world. The road and the automobile brought the desert closer, tore off its shroud of mystery without diminishing its beauty. On the contrary, the beauty created by nature was supplemented by the beauty created by the artistic hands of man. Admiring the pure colors of the desert, its complex and majestic architecture, we never ceased to admire the broad even highway with its silvery bridges, its neatly placed water pipes, its mounds and its dips. Even the gasoline stations that so annoyed us in the East and in the Middle West, here in the desert looked like proud monuments to human might. And the automobile

seemed twice as beautiful in the desert as in the city. Its streamlined, polished surface reflected the sun, and its shadow, deep and sharply lined, fell proudly on the virgin sands.[73]

Ilf and Petrov find the Americans themselves to be hospitable, reliable, sociable, helpful, good workers, and uncomplaining in adversity:

> When we left for America there was one thing we did not take into account—American hospitality. It is boundless, and far outshines any other, including even Russian, Siberian, or Georgian hospitality.[74]

> There are many wonderful and attractive features in the character of the American people. They are superb workers with hands of gold. Our engineers say that working with Americans is sheer pleasure. Americans are accurate, but far from pedantic. They are precise. They know how to keep their word and trust the word of others. They are always ready to come to your assistance. They are good comrades, easygoing people.[75]

Much of the negative side of America for Ilf and Petrov, as with most Soviets, is the seeming preponderance of "bandits," "racketeers," and "bankers"—all of whom they consider one and the same.[76] Adhering to the Marxist premise that capitalism is the root of all evil, they see the profit motive behind almost everything:

> The persistent advertising has conditioned the American to drink juice at breakfast and at lunch. The juice contains vitamins that are very beneficial

for the consumer; but the sale of the juice is beneficial for the fruit growers.[71]

They also believe that the automat was invented not to serve the public better, but to deprive waitresses of their jobs and increase profits.[78]

The authors frankly report their habit of comparing what they saw in America with life in the Soviet Union:

> We constantly talked about the Soviet Union, drew parallels, made comparisons. We noticed that the Soviets whom we often met in America were possessed by the same feelings. There was not a single conversation that did not lead in the end to a reference to the Soviet Union. "We have this." "And we have that." "We could use this." "We do that better." "This we can't do yet." "This we have already mastered." [79]

The objectivity and honesty of this passage is rare in Soviet writings which are usually not disposed to admit that they do not have or would like to acquire something that America already has. They are more inclined to claim that they do everything better. Ilf and Petrov explain their faith in the Communist cause:

> At the foundation of Soviet life lies the Communist idea. We have a definite goal toward which our country is moving. That is why we, people of only moderate achievement in comparison to the Americans, are much calmer and happier than the people of the land of Morgan and Ford, the land of twenty-five million automobiles, of a million and a half miles

of roads, of hot and cold running water, rooms with baths, and service. The slogan that technology solves everything was coined by Stalin after the Communist idea had triumphed. That is why technology does not seem to us an evil genie that cannot be returned to its bottle. On the contrary we want to catch up with American technology and surpass it. America does not know what will happen to it tomorrow. We know and can predict with definite accuracy what will happen with us in fifty years.[80]

It is interesting to compare this passage with Maya-kovsky's arrogant assertion that "Soviets look down upon the bourgeois." Ilf and Petrov explain their feelings without restorting to name calling or inflammatory statements. The simple and grammatical exposition of their thoughts contrasts with the emotional and repetitive banter of propaganda. There is also no feeling of ill will toward America in *One-Storied America*.

In another passage they are a bit idealistic about Soviet patriotism:

Soviets abroad are not merely travelers, engineers, or diplomats. They are all lovers torn away from the object of their love who continually think about it. This is a unique patriotism that cannot be understood, let us say, by an American. The American is probably a good patriot. . . . He asks only one thing of his country—that it leave him alone and not interfere with his listening to the radio or going to the movies. . . . He does not understand the patriotism of a Soviet who loves not a juridical homeland that provides only the laws of government, but a tangible homeland where he owns the land, the factories, the stores, the banks, the dreadnaughts, the airplanes, the theaters and the books, a homeland where he himself is politician and the master of all.[81]

The tone of *One-Storied America* is essentially that of objective reporters in contrast to the polemical tone of Gorky, Mayakovsky, and Pilnyak. This is evidenced in the general lack of emotionality, the absence of satiric hyperbole and stereotypes, and the fact that the authors report the good they saw as well as the bad. While preferring their own country, Ilf and Petrov approach America with open curiosity, explore her from coast to coast, and describe what they find. When criticizing something they usually explain their objections, and seldom indulge in rhetoric or hysteria. Like many visitors to New York they find the city dark and depressing:

> New York is astonishingly beautiful! But why does one feel sad in this great city? The buildings are so high that the sunlight lies only on the upper stories, and throughout the day one has the impression that the sun is setting. A morning sunset. No doubt that is why one feels so sad in New York.[82]

The fault is not proclaimed in emotional exaggeration but rationally explained as an inevitable consequence of closely constructed tall buildings.

However, while marking a new dimension and direction for the Soviet image of America in their *One-Storied America*, Ilf and Petrov also helped to propagate the conventional caricature of capitalism in a little known story, *"Tonya,"* published in the December 1937 issue of *Znamja*. Tonya is a young Soviet girl, newly married, who comes to America with her husband, a junior officer

in the Embassy in Washington, D.C. Tonya's excitement
and happiness are short-lived, however, as she and her
husband fall prey to the capitalist way of life. Medical
expenses deplete their budget when Tonya's husband
finds a society doctor who cures his colds by a $200 ton-
sillectomy. This blow forces them to do without new
winter coats (the authors do not explain why their old
Muscovite coats will not do). They must also forego a
baby carriage and crib, settling for a common cradle
"like those used by the poor Negroes." When the baby
arrives, further hospital expenses all but devastate the
hapless couple. The "moral" that such terrible things
would never have happened in Moscow where such things
are free is repeatedly emphasized. Tonya learns a vivid
and bitter lesson:

> Tonya, who had understood from her Pioneer
> days what capitalism meant, and had even given
> small reports about it at school and in the factory,
> suddenly confronted it in real life. And you can
> imagine how furious she was. The capitalist system
> interfered with her life. Although it was harmful
> for her to get upset, she excitedly cursed this system
> every night.[83]

The pedantic moralizing of this paragraph is clearly addressed to the reader: "And you can imagine how furious
she was."

"Tonya" is so different from *One-Storied America*
in style and in content that it is hard to believe both
works were written by the same authors about the same
country. "Tonya" is completely different from any other
work of Ilf and Petrov as well. It is a poorly written
publicist sketch, full of bathetic distortion that betrays

the craftsmanship of these two literary masters. The work may have been written, or at least finished, by Petrov as it appeared some eight months after the death of Ilf in April of 1937. It may possibly be an attempt to atone for the objectivity of *One-Storied America*. The notes to the latest edition of their works comment on this "new genre" of the writers: "The political school of *Pravda* taught the writers to widen the use of the publicist weapon as a means of satirical denunciation." [84]

The two works contain many discrepancies in their portrayals of the American way of life. For example, the Adamses, not wealthy people, apparently have no difficulty in finding a nursemaid for their two-year-old daughter and taking off for two months to tour America with the authors. Ilf and Petrov repeatedly state how easy, inexpensive, and comfortable it is to travel across America, and how many Americans themselves are on the roads at all hours. They are also continually impressed with American hospitality and helpfulness. In light of these observations it seems a bit strange that Tonya has almost no contact with America outside the Embassy walls and cannot afford a baby sitter for an occasional evening out with her husband.

The moralistic tone and sharply negative portrayal of American life in "Tonya" thus continue the caricature tradition of Gorky, Mayakovsky, and Pilnyak. This interesting dichotomy in Ilf and Petrov's writings on America marks the beginning of a double image of America in Soviet writings. On one hand we have negative caricature that condemns all of America as an ideological enemy. On the other hand we have an objective commentary that reports the good as well as the bad in America. The latter presentation, however, was to lie dormant until the 1960's.

Ilf and Petrov also wrote a humorous sketch on life in America in 1936, "Columbus Moors to the Shore." This is a description of contemporary New York through the eyes of the fifteenth century Columbus, who writes the Spanish King about his new discovery:

I have sailed many seas but never before have I encountered such original natives. They absolutely cannot tolerate quiet. In order to enjoy noise as much as possible, they have constructed special roads on iron stems where iron carriages roll day and night, producing the clamor so beloved by the natives.

I still have not been able to determine whether or not they are cannibals. However, they do eat hot dogs. With my own eyes I saw many eating places that invite passers-by to eat these hot dogs. They even praise their taste.

. . . . .

I have come to the conclusion that the natives are pagans. They have many gods whose names are written in fire on their huts. Their most important gods seem to be the goddess Coca-Cola, the god Drug Store, the goddess Cafeteria and the great god of gasoline fumes, Ford. He seems to be their Zeus.[85]

This work is typical of the imaginative wit of the pair and of the style that made them famous. The satire of Ilf and Petrov is never sarcastic or denigrating but is exercised with the true artist's delicate sense of balance and harmony between form and content. Their satire is derived from a deep love of man, a Horatian satire [86] that stems from the humanist's conception of evil as a moral failing as well as from his desire to help man recognize his weaknesses.

This literary image of America, a creative image conceived in fun, is also new to Soviet literature. And it, too, will vanish for a quarter of a century until an imaginative and perceptive young poet moors to the American shore in the year 1961. Andrei Voznesensky rediscovers America for the Soviet reader, and rediscovers as well the role of the artist as moral conscience rather than political propagandist.

Notes

1. A. Solzhenitsyn, *V kruge pervom* (New York 1968), 150.
2. M. Gorky, "Gorod želtogo d'javola," *Sobranie sočinenij v 18 tomax* (Moscow 1960), IV, 18–27.
3. *New York American,* April 12, 1906, 1.
4. *The World,* April 13, 1906, 6.
5. Filia Holtzman, "A Mission That Failed: Gor'kij in America," *The Slavic and East European Journal,* VI, iii (Fall 1962), 230.
6. M. Gorky, *op. cit.,* 19.
7. *New York American,* April 13, 1906, 4.
8. M. Gorky, *op. cit.,* 21.
9. *Ibid.,* 22.
10. *Ibid.,* 20.
11. *Ibid.*
12. *Ibid.,* 19.
13. *Ibid.,* 20.
14. *Ibid.,* 21.
15. *Ibid.,* 27.
16. M. Gorky, *Sobranie sočinenij v 30 tomax,* XXVIII (Moscow 1954), 422.
17. *Ibid.,* 419.
18. *Ibid.,* 422.
19. *Ibid.,* 423.
20. *Ibid.,* 421.
21. *New York Tribune,* April 21, 1906, 7.
22. V. Mayakovsky, *Ob Amerike* (Moscow 1952).
23. *Ibid.,* 131.
24. *Ibid.,* 143.

25. *Ibid.*, 127.
26. *Ibid.*, 48–50.
27. *Ibid.*, 70–73.
28. *Ibid.*, 62–64.
29. The introduction to a longer, uncompleted poem, "In a Loud Voice," written in 1930, contains a line stating that besides a freshly washed shirt, the poet needs nothing: *"I krome / sveževymyto soročki, / skažu po sovesti, / mne ničego ne nado."*
30. V. Mayakovsky, *op. cit.*, 74–76.
31. *Ibid.*, 121–122.
32. *Ibid.*, 65–69. English translation by George Reavey in *The Bedbug and Selected Poetry*, ed. Patricia Blake (New York 1960), 173–181.
33. *Ibid.*, quoted by Patricia Blake in the Introduction, 15.
34. V. Mayakovsky, *Op. cit.*, 120.
35. *Ibid.*, 46–47.
36. See Nils Åke Nilsson's interesting article on this device, *"Usad'ba noč'ju, čingisxan'*, Verbs Derived from Personal Names as a Means of Expression in Literary Russian," *Lingua Viget*, Festschrift in Honor of V. Kiparsky, (Helinski 1964), 97–101.
37. A line in the final poem of this cycle, *"Domoj"* [Homeward], shows Mayakovsky's awareness of his unpoetic verse: "From the heavens of poetry / I throw myself into Communism." *Op. cit.*, 82.
38. *Ibid.*, 87–88.
39. *"Proščane"* [Farewell] from Mayakovsky's French cycle, *"Pariž."*
40. Quoted in *Istorija russkoj sovetskoj literatury* (3 vols.), I (Moscow 1958), 57.
41. *Novyj mir*, II (February 1933), 258. This passage gives a fair idea of the mood of the times. Socialist realism had been formally declared the only permissible literary doctrine the year before, and nonconformers were ruthlessly pursued.
42. Pilnyak, *O-kèj, amerikanskij roman* (Moscow 1933).
43. *Ibid.*, 187.
44. *Ibid.*, 196.
45. *Ibid.*, 215.
46. *Ibid.*
47. *Ibid.*, 39.
48. *Ibid.*, 53.
49. *Ibid.*, 76.
50. *Ibid.*, 140.
51. *Ibid.*, 167.

52. *Ibid.*, 169. (This is a play on the Slavic folk myth that describes the world as supported on the backs of three whales.)
53. *Ibid.*, 69.
54. *Ibid.*
55. *Ibid.*, 72.
56. *Ibid.*, 123.
57. *Ibid.*, 124.
58. *Ibid.*, 46.
59. *Literaturnaja ènciklopedija*, (11 vols.), VIII (Moscow 1934), 640.
60. I. Ilf and E. Petrov, *Odnoètažnaja Amerika, Sobranie sočinenij v 5 tomax*, IV (Moscow 1961), 7–448.
61. I. Ilf and E. Petrov, "*Tonja,*" *Ibid.*, 451–498.
62. I. Ilf and E. Petrov, "*Kolumb pričalivaet k beregu,*" *op. cit.*, III, 73–81.
63. I. Ilf and E. Petrov, *Odnoètažnaja Amerika*, 100.
64. *Ibid.*, 107.
65. *Ibid.*, 97.
66. The name if not the character portrait of Mr. Adams is fictitious. Ilf and Petrov did travel with an American engineer who had worked for seven years in the Soviet Union. His real name was S. A. Tron. Ilf had written of Mr. Tron to his wife: "This is Pickwick. It is very pleasant and amusing to travel with him." *Ibid.*, 587.
67. *Ibid.*, 394.
68. *Ibid.*, 208–209.
69. *Ibid.*, 337.
70. *Ibid.*, 338.
71. *Ibid.*, 163.
72. *Ibid.*, 240.
73. *Ibid.*, 238.
74. *Ibid.*, 42.
75. *Ibid.*, 241.
76. *Ibid.*, 427.
77. *Ibid.*, 36.
78. *Ibid.*, 37.
79. *Ibid.*, 435.
80. *Ibid.*, 439–440.
81. *Ibid.*, 434–435.
82. *Ibid.*, 442.
83. "*Tonja,*" *Ibid.*, 476.
84. *Ibid.*, 592.
85. "*Kolumb pričalivaet k beregu,*" *op. cit.*, 80.

86. See Gilbert Highet's study, *The Anatomy of Satire* (Princeton 1962), in which he distinguishes two types of satirist:

> There are, then, two main conceptions of the purpose of satire, and two different types of satirist. One likes most people, but thinks they are rather blind and foolish. He tells the truth with a smile, so that he will not repel them but cure them of that ignorance which is their worst fault. Such is Horace. The other type hates most people, or despises them. He believes rascality is triumphant in his world; or he says, with Swift, that though he loves individuals he detests mankind. His aim therefore is not to cure, but to wound, to punish, to destroy. Such is Juvenal. (p. 235)

Part II
The Emergence of a More Positive Image

2.

Discovery: Andrei Voznesensky, Poems

Andrei Voznesensky, born in 1933, is one of the younger generation of Soviet writers, those who began to publish after the Thaw period of 1953–54, and whose work assumed increasing importance during the 1960's. Voznesensky, who studied to be an architect, published his first poems in 1958 and has since become one of the leading poets in the Soviet Union. Although he is not as well known as his contemporary, Yevtushenko, especially in the West where the latter's flamboyant style has attracted much attention, Voznesensky is generally considered to be the better poet in technique, imagination, and innovation. He is also inclined to abstain from political themes.

Voznesensky visited America for the first time during the spring of 1961 with Yevtushenko and several other Soviet writers, and appears to have been enraptured by America. His visit inspired a cycle of creative poems, as well as some prose commentary about various aspects of

American life which were published in a collection entitled *Triangular Pear*.[1] In the introduction to this work
the poet writes:

> I am working on a great theme—the "discovery
> of America." It is based on my American impres-
> sions. But in the process of writing, life, memories
> and landscapes of Russia and the Baltic burst into
> the narrative, diverting the author from his principle
> theme. . . . The poem drowned like an overcrowded
> ship. But alongside it arose an independent or-
> ganism, a "poem of lyrical digressions." Poems re-
> shuffled themselves arbitrarily, outside theme or
> geography, like thoughts in the head.[2]

The poet's epigraph to *Triangular Pear* is "Be a
lyrical attack, / It's a crime to digress!" And the book is
subtitled *Lyrical Digressions from the Poem*. Thus, the
poet thrice serves notice that he allows his imagination
full scope—that his images flow in a stream of consciousness "outside theme or geography, like thoughts in the
head." This use of lyrical digression may be in part a
stylistic device to absolve the poet from having to write
on political themes, and to enable him to say what he
wants about America—to present his personal impressions
from his trip. The epigraph is in part Aesopian.[3] It seems
to contradict the poet's introductory remarks about digressions, noting that it is a "crime" to digress from a
"lyrical attack." This may be in part an awareness that
he will be criticized for his "digressions" from the proper
(according to socialist realism tenets) form and content.
It may also be a cryptographical assertion that his "digressions" are really his "attacks." The Russian contains
some shrewd punning: the words "digression" [*otstu-*

plenie], "attack" [*nastuplenie*] and "crime" [*prestuplenie*] all stem from the same root, differing only in their prefixes. The "drowned poem" thus could be the one he wanted to write but could not for ideological reasons, being forced to "reshuffle" his impressions accordingly. Such Aesopian language, even in prose commentary, is typical of Voznesensky, making the interpretation of some of his poems very difficult.

Voznesensky's poetics is very complicated as well. He delights in sound play, puns, internal rhyme, sharp contrasts, unusual imagery and the casual mixing of slang with abstract words. He also mixes serious thought with lighthearted exposition to a point where it becomes difficult at times to separate the idea from the word play. The poetess Marina Tsvetaeva, whom Voznesensky greatly admires,[4] once observed that the reading of a poem is essentially an unraveling of what lies concealed behind the lines, beyond the bounds of the words.[5] Voznesensky often seems to take special delight in constructing riddles for his readers to unravel. His form and imagery border on the surrealistic at times, further obscuring the meaning of some poems. Perhaps this vagueness is intentional; perhaps it is the result of a search by the poet for new forms of creative expression.

Whatever the poet's intentions and however complex the obscurities, there can be no doubt that Voznesensky presents the Soviet reading public with a refreshingly new image of America, and becomes one of the first Soviet writers since Ilf and Petrov to depart from the standardized negative caricature of American life.

Voznesensky approaches America with a sense of adventure and discovery, like a modern-day Columbus. His goal is not to confirm preconception but to uncover the "naked soul" of America. He plunges directly into the central themes of *Triangular Pear* in his poem "Introductory." [6] One of these themes is the act of uncovering, of seeking the inner core of things. This is seen in the opening words, "Uncover yourself, America!" and in the poet's repetitive use of verbs of strong action that emphasize the uncovering: "rip off," "sweep away," "dive into," "hack away." The poet's tone is resolute:

> Uncover yourself, America!
> Eureka!
> I crown Emelka,
>   as I uncover, sniffing,
> America—in America
> Myself—
>   in myself.
> I rip off the peel from the planet,
>   sweep away dust
>   and decay,
> As I dive
>   into the depth
>   of the matter.

Another theme is the poet as rebel. "Emelka" refers to Emelyan Pugachov, the leader of the 1773 rebellion named for him and a symbol of revolt against repression. Voznesensky seeks to crown or to emulate him. His concept of the artist as rebel seems to be important for him. In another poem, "The Master," he says: "The true born artist / is always a public defender. / In him is the spirit of rebellion / and eternal revolt." [7] And in yet another poem, "The Artist," he refers to artists as "accoucheurs of the new." [8]

The poet is also acutely aware that his attitude may

be frowned upon in the line "Is the artist hooliganizing?" [*Xudožnik xuliganit?*], which also provides a good example of his ear for alliterative play. And he was considered a "hooligan" of sorts: one Soviet critic later characterized this collection as a "blind imitation of modern decadent art." [9]

Like Columbus, Voznesensky follows his intuition: "Frolic, / Columbus! / Intuitively / I sweep toward shore." This line also stresses the poet's subjective approach to America: no maps, no charts. no prejudices. The latter is alluded to at the end of the poem: "Seeking / India / You find / America!" In other words, the explorer does not always find what he expects. There is also a Russian idiom, *otkrytie Ameriki,* literally, the "discovery of America," but figuratively implying the discovery of something already well known. This poem may be in part an intentional pun on that idiom, hinting at the poet's discovery of an America divested of her propaganda-formed image, a "new" America—that was already there. But the poet is not concerned solely with America here. He is also seeking his own inner core: "America—in America, / Myself— / in myself."

The image of a triangular pear is an expressive one. It seems to be an abstract symbol representing the poet's interest in the *essence* of things, and is possibly derived from the old Cubist preoccupation with form and essence.[10] The poet writes in notes included in this collection:

What is important to me in poetry? —A glance into the soul of man, into myself, into inner-consciousness. Not into the external form.

Form should be clear, unfathomably disquieting, full of higher meaning—like the sky in which only radar can detect the presence of an airplane.[11]

The "triangular" pear becomes a "trapezoidal" fruit: two related yet different abstractions of the pear[12] which reflect the strong sense of motion pervading much of Voznesensky's poetry. "The spiral is the symbol of movement, and if you will, of life," he writes.[13] Life is continually changing for Voznesensky, and one must plunge into the flow of life to catch even part of its essence. At the same time it must be remembered that the abstraction is but one expression of the pear's essence. It is not meant as an all-embracing confinement, but as a subtle projection to stimulate the radar of man's mind.

The poet takes the fruit not to devour it, but to seek its inner core, to discern its essence which, having been uncovered, will light up like an altar. The word "altar" carries implications of sacredness, the sacred essence of life that seems to be one of the poet's greatest concerns. The image of a "triangular pear"—the title of this collection as well—may thus be a symbol for the "naked soul" that the poet seeks: in America, in himself and in life. Tangential to his interest in the essence of things is the poet's awareness that lies or outward appearances do not alter the truth: "Let them lie that it's emerald, / your melon is crimson red."

Voznesensky's form and many of his images in "Introductory" are subtle and elusive, and the reader has great difficulty in correctly attuning the radar of his intuition to discover the poet's thoughts. The poem as a whole seems not so much about America as a personal statement by the poet about the need for an undogmatic search for the truth, and a readiness to accept whatever may be found. As far as America is concerned, however, the poem may be interpreted as a statement of the poet's intended approach to America, to which he willingly gives the same respectful attention he pays everything he meets. This is a profoundly new attitude toward America among

Soviet writers, who have previously come mainly to confirm the Party's negative propaganda with their written words. A Soviet critic, V. Nazarenko, noted this sharp departure from the publicist writings of other Soviet poets,[14] and expressed his displeasure over Voznesensky's "digression" from Communism's ideological battle in art.[15]

But Voznesensky sees a different America, a much more complex, three-dimensional and hard-to-define America. The poet comments on the multiplicity and the elusiveness of America's "naked soul" in other poems from this cycle, among which is one entitled "Yet Another Introductory." [16] In this poem the poet chases the spirit of America like a greyhound, hoping to grasp her soul, searching for a "triangular pear" to provide him with an abstract exposition of her essence. But this eludes him: "I nearly caught up, / but you coolly eluded pursuit." An advance apology for any misunderstanding follows: "Read and forgive, / if something in the turmoil I've not understood." This is perhaps the highest possible expression of respect, and nowhere else in Soviet writings has such a personal comment been addressed to America. Communist dogma does not permit agnostic speculation.

New York itself is briefly but positively described in the first and last lines of "Yet Another Introductory." The first couplet, "I adore / your flaming floors, soaring to the gates of paradise" is an expression of wonder over the buildings. Voznesensky is speaking as an architect as well as an observer, so his compliment is twofold. He also writes of his admiration for New York's Guggenheim Museum, an edifice that reminds him of an exhibition pavillion he himself had designed around a similar spiral concept while still an architecture student:

The museum itself is a work of art. Matisse's fruity brush strokes and Klee's mirages have finally found a suitable frame. The walls of the museum are slightly concave so that the pictures hang without touching the walls, as though they were suspended in mid-aid. The spiral is a symbol of motion, and if you will, of life.[17]

And the last couplet of the poem compares the sun of New York to a ladybug [*bož'ja-korovka*]. The Russian expression is a very tender one, but again, the poet leaves us with an ambiguous and elusive image.

Voznesensky has also captured the contrasting sides of America with wit and ingenuity in lines such as "Coca-Cola. Carillons." [*Koka-kola. Kolokola.*] The rhythm, alliteration, and internal rhyme, as well as the effect of the line's simplicity, are lost in translation. Such punning is a device used with frequency and abandon by Voznesensky, who seems to delight in sound play. In the previous line as well the alliteration is striking in Russian: *"Po bezbožnoj, / bejsbol'noj, / po benzoopasnoj Amerike"* [Through Godless, / baseball-fan-full, / benzine-fumed America].

The first poem in *Triangular Pear*, "New York Night Airport," [18] is actually an ode to Kennedy International Airport. The poem is an enthusiastic reaction to a creation of twentieth-century technological man. The poet seems to identify with the soul of the airport as his discerning architect's eye appraises its composition and structure, and finds them pleasing. He sees in it his own self-portrait: "My self-portrait, neon retort, apostle of the heavenly gates." The poet contrasts the mass of insignificant people given new dignity as "arrivals" with the powerful airplane, ruler of the skies, that is, however, dependent on the earth below to "let it land." The description of a plane at night as a cigarette flickering in the dark is highly imaginative and illustrative of the

freshness of Voznesensky's imagery. His grasp of the irony
of life is displayed in the next part of the poem, "The
Interior," where he notes that even governments uncon-
cernedly subordinate themselves to the will of the Traffic
Controller, whose "mighty eye" looks out on this other
world of the sky like a "crystal monster-creature."

There is also ambivalence in Voznesensky's attitude
toward this modern world, ambivalence expressed in the
next line, "Sweet, yet pitiful, to be a son of the future."
The poet is somewhat wary of the technological age, yet
he feels completely at home in it. He sees unlimited
possibilities for man in scientific accomplishment, and
looks forward to the future. In an interview with Olga
Carlisle, Voznesensky said:

> "The second half of the 20th century is the most
> magnificent time of all to be alive in! Paradoxically,
> the Atomic Age has put within our reach the brother-
> hood of man. The atomic scientist has broken down
> the natural world to its particles; it is up to the poet
> to recreate its unity" [19]

Voznesensky does not lament the passing of the old way
of life, symbolized in part by the "wedding-cake station,"
a reference to the ornate train stations of the early part
of the century. Not ornament but function determines the
structure of an airport, and the poet feels at one with
this airport that controls the heavens. The Brooklyn
Bridge that so impressed Mayakovsky is a poor comparison: "The monument of the era's / An airport." This
poem is mainly descriptive, the poet's personal impression of a modern American airport. The imagery is
original and the tone is fervent, making the poem a

significant contribution toward a new Soviet conception of America—the creative writer's *personal* vision of the land.

It is interesting to note that Nazarenko takes Voznesensky literally when he says the airport is his self-portrait, and interprets the images of the "mighty eye looking out on another world" and the "embassy accredited for ozone and sunshine" as vivid metaphors for the poet himself. He advances the theory that the entire cycle of poems about America is an allegorical assertion of the poet's search for "myself in myself." [20] There may well be some substance to this interpretation. There is evidence that other writers, notably Kataev and Yevtushenko, may be using America as an allegorical search for themselves.

Besides taking note of the positive side of America, Voznesensky initiates a completely new approach to her unfavorable side. The tone of his poem "Striptease" [21] is not the gleeful tone of an exposé of America's misfortunes, but an expression of sadness over the "scale of the universe." The poet describes what he sees with a deep sense of anguish over the existence of such vulgarity in life, but he does not moralize and he does not equate the stripper with America. Indeed, to dispel the possibility of such an interpretation, he adds the line: "You're America? like an idiot I ask her." The word "idiot" implies the banality, and possibly also the untruth inherent in such a question. The last two lines change the subject, thus eliminating the need for a direct answer by the poet. This ambiguity in itself is a positive sign, and Voznesensky's humanistic approach to America is one that will be followed by Nekrasov and Kataev in their travel memoirs.

Among the poems on America in this early collection is one that is completely surrealistic, "A New York Bird." [22]

This poem is something quite new for Soviet poetry in general and may have influenced the style of Valentin Kataev's surrealistic story, *The Sacred Well*, in part an account of his visit to America that will be discussed below. The image of an aluminum bird with a woman's face is an almost Chagallian figure brought up to date for the technological age. Voznesensky again seems to be alluding to the elusiveness of the "spirit" of America as he strives to communicate with this strange apparition: "Who are you? a cybernetic delirium? / half-robot? half-spirit?" This humorous characterization of America's two halves: technology (commercialism) and spirit (soul) was also noted in "Yet Another Introductory" in the line "Coca-Cola. Carillons." The images in the next couplet continue the surrealistic wit: "a crossbreed of a queen of the blues / and a flying saucer?" The Russian contains an ingenious alliterative rhyme, *bliuza* [of the blues] and *bliudca* [saucer], that is typical of Voznesensky's inventive poetics, and is yet another example of the poet's word play that must be kept in mind when seeking to interpret some of his images. Sound, not necessarily sense, is often the source of his imagery, as it is with Boris Pasternak.

The strange apparition is both hard ("with a cigarette between your teeth") and soft (the eyes remind him of a girl in Chicago). The next lines ("she had such puffed-up / gassy pouches under the eyes") convey a very tender image in Russian, partially due to the virtually untranslatable diminutive *"sinjački."* The poet seems to feel a sense of identity with this apparition of America: "Something strange from the outside / surges up in me / as in a connecting vessel"—the sensation is not unpleasant. As in "Striptease" his eager questioning ("Will you tell me what you know?") remains unanswered when he is interrupted and the poem abruptly ends. Despite the delirious apparitions, the tone of the poem is not apprehensive. The lines about a sleeping friend (Yevtushenko?) break the tension caused by the apparition and provide comic relief: "Wrapped in a capitalist sheet / My friend sleeps." The lines seem to imply that even Communists can sleep well in capitalist sheets: there's really nothing to fear. Such light treatment of a nightmare may be a good-natured spoof of the American monster myth as well as an exercise in a new idiom that conveys the poet's impression of an elusive America in the surrealistic language so befitting the 1960's.

The alienation of some of the youth in America is described in another poem, "Digression in the Rhythm of Rock 'n Roll." [23] The poem seems to be a series of disconnected impressions of the world of the rock 'n rollers, portrayed as a world of despair and threatened disintegration:

> We're the products of atomic disintegration.
> We're the pay-off
>   for our fathers' dissipation.
> Instead of TVs, we'll get gas ovens.
> In the howl of motorbikes and cattle
> Our bacchanalias are dread, like wakes.
> Rock, rock—
>   a dance of doom!

The poem ends in a frenzied tone:

> From the Andes to the Atlantic,
> All neonized from tears,
> Our youth
>   ("oh, only not her, Rock Rock, she's not yet
>   seventeen!")

Our youth strains like a lunatic.
Rock! Rock!
SOS! SOS!

The word "rock" in Russian [*rok*] also means a barren fate. Thus, there is an ominous play on the double meaning of this word. This same theme of alienation is presented in another poem from the American cycle, "Digressions in the Form of Beatniks' Monologues": [24]

With rocket-dromes reverberating,
                        with atomic rain pouring,
The times spat at me.
I spit at the times!
Politics? What's the use of agitating!
                        Civilization is suffocating.

It is interesting to note that the theme of atomic disintegration becomes an important leitmotif in Kataev's work *The Sacred Well*. In Voznesensky's poem it is a metaphor for the threatened retribution of disillusioned youth who "spit at the times": "My demonism—like dynamite / Having ripened, will reduce you to ashes."

The second monologue of this poem is subtitled "Revolt of the Machines," and deals with the estrangement of the human being in the technological age, "enslaved by the machines we man." This illustrates the other half of Voznesensky's ambivalent attitude toward the modern age. As we have seen in some of his other poems and notes, he seems enthusiastic about modern science and its possibilities for achieving the brotherhood of man. Here we see him taking seriously his poet's role as a guardian of man's soul—seeking to recreate the unity of the natural world by warning man against the improper use of his technological knowledge:

> O plundering things of the era!
> A veto is laid on our soul.
> We retreat into the mountains and into beards,
>
> > We plunge naked into the water,
> > But the rivers are growing shallow, or
> > The fishes are dying in the seas.
> >
> > Women give birth to Rolls Royces.
> > Radiation!

This theme reappears in the later poem, "OZA" (Part IV):

> Will the trochee, silver flutist, perish
> as trout have died when blocked by river dams?
> > . . . . .
> And why, forgetting meadow, pine and grove,
> are we drawn to poems as to herbs for curing scurvy?
> Then, shyly in us, souls flower in joy.
> But robots,
> > robots,
> > > robots,
> cut short our speech.
> > . . . . .
> No time to think, no time
> in offices, as in coal trams,
> there's only gross and net—
> no time to be a man!
> > . . . . .
> We're being disemployed, O heart.
> The world is turning robot.
> How horrible! Mama,
> > > bear me back—back into the
> > > womb![25]

But for all this seeming despair, "OZA" goes on to reaffirm Voznesensky's basic optimism in a prose passage:

"I think of the future," the historian continues, "when all dreams will be realized. In good hands technology is good. To fear technology? That's to go back to the cave!"

The poet seems to identify with the beatniks in their "Monologue," so the poem may be not only about American youth. Voznesensky rarely addresses his lyrics to specific nationalities. He writes about mankind in general, Communist as well as capitalist, and avoids the use of these labels except in jest. The recurrence of the theme of alienation in other poems shows that he sees it as a phenomenon not unique to the West.

One poem in *Triangular Pear* is about the American Negroes, "Digression for Voice and Drums—Negroes Sing." [26] The alliterative rhythm of the poem is striking from the very first words: *"My—tamtamy gomeričnye s glazami goremyčnymi, klubimsja, kak dymy my."* [We beat our Homeric drums with wretched eyes, raising clouds of dust, we.] The internal rhyme (*tamtami/glazami; gomeričnye/goremyčnymi*) as well as the alteration of three- and five-syllable words accented on the middle syllable create a most effective drum-like rhythm. The uneven meter throughout the poem continues the onomatopoeic effect, vividly capturing the beat of African drums.

The reference in the first line to "Homeric drums," and the line "We are Negroes, we are poets" give rise to a possible allegorical interpretation for this poem: the Negro as a metaphor for the poet in the Soviet Union. Nazarenko seems to feel that this is the poem's true meaning.[27] However, Voznesensky may just have been intrigued by the rhyme possibilties of the words "Homeric" [*gomeričnoe*] and "wretched" [*goremyčnoe*]. The powerful imagery of the poem, as well as its relentless beat, does communicate the poet's strong feelings of identification with the people in whose name he writes—be they Negroes, poets, or oppressed people of any time or place. The final stanza reaches a climax as the meter switches to simple but forceful iambic tetrameter. The message is rather forcibly expressed as well: "When they kick us about, / The firmament rebels. / Under your boots / The Universe yells!"

Another poem with possible allegorical content is "An Obligatory Digression."[28] This poem is a caricature of the machinations of secret police agents, ostensibly from the American FBI. The poet describes the omnipresent bugging devices: "Hotels have ears, / The showerhead's a mike. / And the urinal stares at us, / Like the eye of a plaster goddess." He is pursued by "17 brows from the FBI" who record his actions with their cameras, each capturing a different Voznesensky. The poet feels torn apart, deprived of his being: "But somehow there's no me left in me." He also strongly resents this invasion of his privacy: "It's unbearable to be crucified, / transparent to each birthmark."

The title of the poem is in itself noteworthy—the poet feels an *obligation* to protest such vulgar intrusions into the sanctity of human life. There is a possibility that Voznesensky may also be commenting in this poem on the activities of the Soviet internal security agents whose slang name *"stukači"* is used at the beginning as well as the end of the poem. The theme of citizen surveillance is one that will reappear rather less ambiguously in the American writings of Nekrasov and Kataev.

The December 1962 visit of then Premier Kruschchev

to an exhibition of abstract art in the Manezh Gallery in Moscow resulted in the immediate closing of the exhibition and the unleashing during 1963 of a bitter campaign against abstractionism in art and literature. Voznesensky was one of the writers singled out for harsh criticism by Khrushchev for failing in his duty as a writer as well as for improper comportment on his trips abroad. Called upon to repent and change his ways, Voznesensky promised only that he would remember the Premier's words and work hard to write sincere poetry. He went into semiexile and traveled through the hinterlands of the Soviet Union for several months. In the fall of 1963, after writing *"Lonžjumo,"* a long poem in praise of Lenin, Voznesensky was allowed to publish another collection of his poems. *Antimiry* appeared in 1964 and contained the Lenin poem as well as another poem written during the difficult year of 1963, "Monologue of Marilyn Monroe." [29]

This poem seems to express the protest of the individual against the heartless indifference of the times, a theme found in many of Voznesensky's poems. It is brillantly written, constructed around the repetition of two key words: "unbearable" [*nevynosimo*] and "suicide" [*samoubijstvo*]. The rhyme and punning in Russian are extraordinary. In the first stanza, the words "heroine" and "heroin" reflect this even in English:

> I am Marilyn, Marilyn.
>   I am a heroine
> of suicide and heroin.
> For whom are my dahlias flaming?

The Russian words, *geroinja* and *geroina,* find an additional alliterative rhyme in the word for "dahlias," *geor-*

giny—another example of the poet's fascination with the sound of words.

The poem is written in the name of the actress and echos the tone of despair noted in Voznesensky's beatnik poems:

> Unbearable to live thoughtlessly,
> more unbearable—to delve deeper.
> Where are our plans? They've blown us apart,
> existence is suicide,
>
> suicide to battle with trash,
> suicide to make peace with them,
> unbearable, when talentless,
> when talented—more unbearable.

The despair of Marilyn here becomes almost an expression of collective despair. Again, Voznesensky's images and poetics are very complex, and very hard to decipher. One stanza seems to plead for recognition of the *human being* behind the façade of stardom:

> unbearable, this naked posing
> in all the papers, all the posters,
> forgetting
>   that a heart is in the center.

The poet then extends the suicide image from the actress to the world at large, culminating in a "universal Hiroshima"—a woeful spiritual climax mindful of the mood of his beatnik poems:

Suicides—motorcyclists,
suicides rushing to drunkenness,
ministers paling before flashbulbs—
suicides,
      suicides,
the universal Hiroshima approaches,
unbearable,
unbearable waiting till
                everything bursts,
                            above all—
unexplainably unbearable

The surrealism of the imagery here stems in part from the complexity of the poet's alliterative word play in Russian:

Samoubijcy—motociklisty,
samoubijcy spešat upit'sja,
ot vspyšek blicev bledny ministry—
samoubijcy,
        samoubijcy,
idet vsemirnaja Xirosima,
nevynosimo,
nevynosimo vse ždat'
                čtob grjanulo,
                        a glavnoe—
neob"jasnimo nevynosimo

Note the fourfold repetition of *samoubijcy,* in assonantal play with the sounds *sty-spy-stry,* as well as the rhymes *Xirosima/nevynosimo* and *neob"jasnimo/nevynosimo.*

Attacks by the critics for excessive experimentation with complicated forms and obscurity of content continued sporadically until 1966, when they abated somewhat. Voznesensky was even nominated for the coveted

Lenin Prize that spring. For some reason, no prizes were awarded in literature or drama in 1966, but the poet was once again allowed to travel abroad. Voznesensky visited America for the second time in the spring of 1966 on a three-week poetry reading tour which he repeated in the spring of 1967. These two trips have produced only a few poems, although there is evidence that the poet is working on a new American cycle entitled "Walkie-Talkie."

Two poems from this cycle were published during 1967. The first one, "Monologue with Footnotes," [30] is a long poem recalling memories of America. The poem is constructed around the word "peace" [*mir*] which becomes the central theme of the work. The poet enumerates his memories of people and of places in America, and wishes them all peace. The poem opens with the words:

> Peace
> to your ashes,
>   enlightened president.
> I shall understand much,
> sitting until nightfall.
> I shall remove my cap
> and say, "Peace to all."

The last couplet offers a striking contrast to some lines in one of Mayakovsky's poems about America, "Broadway," in which the poet says he is ecstatic over New York, but he refuses to doff his cap to her since Soviets are proud and look down upon the bourgeois. Voznesensky, on the contrary, underlines his intentions to continue his attitude of sympathy and love for America. He may also

be responding to the critic Nazarenko, who earlier chided
him for not following Mayakovsky's example, citing those
very lines of the earlier poet.[31]
One of the "footnotes" in this poem is in itself a
short poem to San Francisco comparing the city of hills
to Kolomenskoe, a hill outside Moscow on which stands
the brilliant white Church of the Ascension, an architectural landmark:

San Francisco is Kolomenskoe,
A light in the midst of a hill,
As high as well water
is cold.

I love you, San Francisco.
Webbed frontispieces
Overbrimming with height
Disappear above me.

At night the foggy cubicles
Fill with gold
Like translucent smokers
Inhaling dangerous red smoke.

It is remorse for the betrayal
Of my youthful dreams,
Cut out from the heavens
And pinned to the bridges.

My architectural youth!
I light my cigarette from your fire
Compressing my lips, pale from love,
Inhaling as deeply as possible.

Down by the hotel, black limousines
Are lined up like shoes—
As if angels
                had flown away
Leaving their galoshes behind.

We are not angels.
The customs dandy
Stamped my visa without even a sound.
Sigh for me,
                San Francisco.
Kolomenskoe, sigh.

The poet candidly expresses his admiration for the city of San Francisco. He sees her bridges as embodiments of the architectural dreams of his youth (like his plans for a Guggenheim-like exhibition hall). The imagery of the poem is striking in its freshness and its expressiveness: the unusual simile comparing height to the coldness of well water, the original metonymy for skyscrapers as "webbed frontispieces" disappearing overhead, the charming image of "angels' galoshes" for black limousines— all show Voznesensky's creative imagination at work. The "customs dandy" may be a metaphor for the spirit of creation that with seeming unconcern stamps the life visas of men, or he may be just the customs man who stamps passports. The poet addresses San Francisco as "thou," the intimate form he always uses with America. His plea to both San Francisco and Kolomenskoe to "sigh" for him might indicate a feeling of aloneness in the poet, a feeling that is reflected in parts of the larger poem as well: "I, too, am someone's / shoe, I feel the Unknown / who wears me."

Other lines in the body of the main poem refer

directly to Voznesensky's unique relationship with America:

> Peace blessed ship
> That discovered America!
> I helped America
> Discover my Russian tongue.

The poet seems to be playing again with words and meaning here, comparing Columbus' discovery of America with America's discovery of his poetry through his many public readings:

> In a high-pitched voice,
> I was the first to sound
> The music of Russia
> In public arenas.
>
> I strain not my voice, but my heart.
> America—you are rhythm.

The above lines affirm the poet's sincerity in reaching out to America. The poem is a collage of impressions—of America and of life, and is dedicated to the American poet Robert Lowell. It is not as cohesively assembled as some of his earlier poems about America, but its tone is peaceful and sincere.

Another poem from the "Walkie-Talkie" cycle, "Strip-tease on Strike," [32] is a good-natured spoof of an event that the poet witnessed in New York, when the strip-teasers were indeed on strike. Most of the poem humorously describes the antics of the strippers striking for their rights: "Social security, a commission on applause, and early pensions—as in the air corps." But the poet gradually extends the theme of "nakedness on strike" to a metaphysical level. The last two stanzas get down to the bare facts of another, more important strike—the strike of truth:

> Truth is on strike. Naked for ages,
> It is no longer printed. And if it is printed,
> It is covered over a hundred times, disguised by
> fig-leaf phrases.
> Just try to pluck it out!
> In cities the earth is covered with asphalt,
> The world wants nakedness,
> nakedness,
> nakedness!
> The world has a devil of an appetite.
> Striptease is on strike.
> It will win!

The development of more important themes within lighthearted subject matter is characteristic of Voznesensky, and the double meaning of the poem provides a good example of one device the younger poets have worked out to express their protests against things they are not permitted to protest openly. Yevtushenko, as we shall see, has mastered this allegorical technique.

Voznesensky visited America for the third time in the spring of 1967 on a second reading tour. An additional scheduled appearance at a Poetry Evening in Philharmonic Hall in New York that June was canceled at the last moment by the Soviet authorities, apparently to punish the poet for his outspoken support of Solzhenitsyn's petition for loosening of censorship restrictions and publication privileges for his and others' works. Voznesensky's continued conciliatory gestures towards America and his continued ignoring of the "ideological struggle" between Russia and America may also have influenced the authorities who canceled his appearance.

Only one poem about America has appeared in print since. "New York Buttons" [33] is about the contemporary vogue, especially among the hippies of Greenwich Village, for wearing metal buttons with various expressions of protest. The poem is exceedingly complex in its imagery, but it clearly seems to consider this kind of protest somewhat superficial. Slogans such as "Make Love Not War," "People Are the Ancestors of Apes," and the like seem irresponsible in face of some of the real problems confronting man today:

> Hooligans! Hooligans!
> Better to suck your thumbs
> than to grow sour like snipe
> in the bourgeois swamps.

The most important thought in the poem seems to be "The contemporary God is irony"—which the poet repeats twice:

> The contemporary God is irony.
> Buttons glisten over a yawn—
> the more horrible, the funnier.
> Like targets for bullets.

The poet seems puzzled by the inanity of some of the hippies' protest. Here again rhyme and alliteration play a role in the selection of the words "horrible" [strašnoe], "funny" ⎣*smešnoe*⎦, and "target" [*mišen'*]. The ending of the poem is completely surrealistic:

> O, autumn, and aspen circles.
> O, eight
> plates abandoned by a juggler,
>   dying momentarily in mid-air,
> as if a giraffe ran away
>   leaving her spots
>   behind.
> The giraffe is astonished—
> in buttons, affixed like
> poisonous red mushrooms to her spine:
> "Make Love Not War."

As mentioned earlier, Voznesensky's sound play sometimes obscures his content (in the first lines "autumn" [*osen'*], "aspen" [*osinovyoe*], and "eight" [*vosem'*] rhyme). His images are usually powerful, condensed impressions of life but are inclined to be elusive before analysis.

The death of Robert Kennedy in June of 1968 prompted the writing of another poem, "June—1968," [34] which is notable for its apoliticism, frankly stated:

> Perhaps I do not understand
> the politics of others,
> but I do understand
> a helpless cheek covered with blood.

Voznesensky, who had visited Kennedy in New York during his 1967 trip, goes on to associate him with Sergei Esenin, a beloved Russian poet who also met a violent death. This is an especially warm reference for a political leader of a capitalist country.

Thus, the young poet Andrei Voznesensky has indeed been a new Columbus: he has discovered a new America in his poems. Reaching out to America as a human being, he has discovered that America, too, is human. She is mortal and fallible; but she has a soul. Voznesensky reverses the Soviet image of America—he looks up at her skyscrapers instead of looking down upon her slums. His values are not ideological, but moral and ethical. His poems are not about the temporal struggle between Communism and capitalism, but about the eternal battle between good and evil, between truth and falsehood, between the noble and the vulgar in man. This is reflected in his concern with the inner nature of things, not with their external forms. True to his initial disassociation from external form, he has not described the appearance of America so much as he has tried to delve into her psyche. Thus his poems are impressions rather than descriptions. His inventive style, while often complex and elusive, has captured some of the contemporary moods, sights, and sounds of America which are themselves often elusive and complex.

In an interview in 1966 Voznesensky himself discusses his discovery of America:

In European eyes, Americans have always appeared as a kind of caricature, which I'm afraid is reflected in our magazines and periodicals. We tend to think of you as a race of cowboys wearing striped shirts and vulgar loud shoes, which are absolutely necessary that you put up on the table, while aggressively chewing your gum, and wearing your hair down over your eyebrows because you simply don't have a forehead. The first thing that struck me was the subdued and tasteful colors of your people's dress.

The first American I spoke to, asking directions,
didn't hook me by the arm and shout slang in my
ear, but seemed very gracious and hospitable. So
were most of the people I met.

. . . . .

Yes, I was truly astonished and moved by the
way Americans can listen to poetry, wholly absorbed,
concentrating as if savoring every word. Everywhere
I found Americans of intellect with keen sensitivity,
a deep and refined soul.
This has been my discovery of America![35]

Voznesensky's discovery of America as a three-dimensional entity, as a complex intermixture of good and
bad, is reflected in the writings of other Soviet writers.
Victor Nekrasov and Valentine Kataev have continued
Voznesensky's unideological approach and humanistic
tone. Kataev has followed his elusive surrealistic style as
well. And Yevgeny Yevtushenko has fallen in love with
America and undergone a transfiguration of his own.

Notes

1. A. Voznesensky, *Treugol'naja gruša* (Moscow 1962). Hereafter
   abbreviated in notes: *T.g.*
2. Vosnesensky's comments find an interesting correspondence in
   the following remark of Pablo Picasso (whom the poet subsequently visited on one of his trips to France): "I put everything
   I like in my pictures. No matter about things, they can simply
   arrange themselves as they see fit." (Quoted in *The Art of
   Painting in the Twentieth Century,* ed. Pierre Seghers, New
   York, 1965, 139.)
3. "Aesopian" is a term widely used by Soviet critics to accuse
   writers of cryptography.
4. Voznesensky once mentioned Tsvetaeva, Mikhail Bulgakov, and
   Valentin Kataev as three Soviet authors who exercise a power-

ful influence on the young Soviet writers of today. *(New York Times,* April 30, 1967, 80.) There is also much of Tsvetaeva's poetics in Voznesensky's work.

5. M. Tsvetaeva, *Izbrannye proizvedenija* (Moscow 1965), 49.
6. A. Voznesensky, *op. cit.,* 11–12.
7. A. Voznesensky, *Antimiry* (Moscow 1964), 207.
8. A. Vosnesensky, *Mozaika* (Moscow 1960), 29.
9. N. Rodičev, *Literatura i žizn',* No. 49, April 25, 1962, 3.
10. It is interesting to compare the following excerpts from *Du Cubisme* of Albert Gleizes and Jean Metzinger, the first Cubist theoreticians (quoted in Seghers, *op. cit.,* 133–134):

> An object has not one absolute form: it has many: it has as many as there are planes in the region of perception. . . . We seek the essential, but we seek it in our personality and not in a sort of eternity, laboriously divided by mathematicians and philosophers. . . . If so many eyes contemplate an object, there are so many images of that object; if so many minds comprehend it, there are so many essential images.

11. A. Voznesensky, *T.g.,* 73.
12. Similar to the geometrical configurations in Picasso's still lifes, for example. It might also be mentioned that Voznesensky himself paints. Though we do not know what style he favors, we may surmise from his interest in abstract expression that his canvases may be abstract as well.
13. A. Voznesensky, *T.g.,* 43.
14. V. Nazarenko, *"Nastuplenie ili otstuplenie?" Zvezda,* July 1962, 186.
15. *Ibid.,* 188.
16. A. Voznesensky, *T.g.,* 13–14.
17. *Ibid.,* 43.
18. *Ibid.,* 7–10.
19. O. Carlisle, "A Rider on the New Wave of Russian Poets," *New York Times Book Review,* October 13, 1963, 52.
20. V. Nazarenko, *op. cit.,* 184.
21. A. Voznesensky, *T.g.,* 15–16.
22. *Ibid.,* 22–23.
23. *Ibid.,* 90–94.
24. *Ibid.,* 38–41.
25. English translation by George Reavey, *The New Russian Poets, 1953 to 1966* (New York 1966), 205–211.
26. A. Voznesensky, *T.g.,* 20–21.
27. V. Nazarenko, *op. cit.,* 184.
28. A. Voznesensky, *T.g.,* 49–52.

29. A. Voznesensky, *Antimiry*, 6–9.
30. A. Voznesensky, *"Monolog s primečanijami,"* *Izvestia*, January 18, 1967, 4.
31. V. Nazarenko, *op. cit.*, 186.
32. A. Voznesensky, *"Zabastovka striptiza,"* *Literaturnaja gazeta*, March 22, 1967, 14.
33. A. Voznesensky, *"N'ju-jorkskie znački,"* *Komsomol'skaja pravda*, June 16, 1968, 3.
34. A. Voznesensky, *"Ijun'—1968,"* *ibid.*
35. L. Banta, "A Chat with Voznesensky," *American Dialogue*, VI (November-December 1966), 11–12.

3.

Observation: Victor Nekrasov,
On Both Sides of the Ocean

Victor Nekrasov, born in 1911, belongs to the middle
generation of Soviet writers, those who began their writing careers during World War II. Like Voznesensky, he
attended the Architecture Institute before turning to a
literary career. Nekrasov's first novel, *In the Trenches
of Stalingrad* (1946), a work based on his war experiences,
received the Stalin Prize for literature in 1947. Nekrasov
excels in the essay [*očerk*], a genre in which the author
can be narrator of his own unfictionalized experience
and observations. He is more interested in the everyday
lives of people and their relationships to one another
than in elaborate plot construction. Even in his fictionalized narrative his plots are minimal. His most recent
fiction work, *Kira Georgievna* (1961), is about the reunion
of a talented sculptor and her student lover twenty years
after he was arrested and imprisoned in a Stalinist labor
camp. Nekrasov is the first Soviet writer to deal with
the reactions of an innocent victim of Stalin's purges.

It is this same personal tone that makes his travel memoirs on America so interesting and revealing.

Nekrasov visited America for two weeks with a group of Soviet tourists in November 1960, but his travel notes on this trip did not appear until two years later. *On Both Sides of the Ocean*[1] is a two-part essay on his trips to Italy and America. It continues some of the new content and stylistic trends we noted in Voznesensky's writings on America, and includes some critical commentary on Soviet life within the travel memoir itself. The somewhat discontinuous narrative style here might be considered a prose variation of Voznesensky's "digressions." However, Voznesensky's image of a multifaceted, modern, and elusive America is conveyed in a modern and often elusive idiom, while Nekrasov's image of America is portrayed in simple and direct language. Voznesensky's surrealism and ambiguity are not to be found in Nekrasov (though they will reappear in Kataev's writings).

Nekrasov's first foreign travel memoir, *First Acquaintance*,[2] about his trip to a writers' conference in Italy in April 1957, may have begun the trend toward personalized and subjective reporting on Western countries among Soviet travelers. Nekrasov is critical of the ways of Western capitalism in *First Acquaintance* (an attitude that is not found in his later work), but he gives an informative and informal account of his trip. His second essay about Italy, covering a two-week trip in March 1962 to another writers' conference, appeared as the first part of *On Both Sides of the Ocean* in the November 1962 issue of *Novyj mir*—the same famous issue that contained Solzhenitsyn's *One Day in the Life of Ivan Denisovich*. This Italian essay is notable for some rather sharp criticisms of Soviet life and behavior which are dispersed throughout the travel commentary on Italy, as well as for its relative abstention from criticism of the West.

Nekrasov's essay on America appeared as the second part of *On Both Sides of the Ocean* in the December issue of *Novyj mir,* and continued the critical digressions noted in the first essay. It may be significant that Nekrasov waited two years to publish his essay on America. He also reversed the chronological sequence of these two trips by writing first about his visit to Italy—although that took place a year and a half after the American trip. The inclusion in the first essay of some commentary about the American trip suggests that the essay on Italy is in part a careful preparation for the essay on America. This partial camouflage, as well as the diversionary sensation over Solzhenitsyn's story, no doubt helped to postpone Soviet reaction to Nekrasov's essay on America. But his work was not overlooked. On January 20, 1963, *Izvestia* carried an unsigned article severely criticizing Nekrasov for his "bourgeois objectivism." In March, members of the Writers' Union accused him of political immaturity and "ideological indecency." Khrushchev also singled him out for sharp criticism in his March 8 speech, and in June he suggested that Nekrasov be expelled from the Party.

However, these attacks subsided somewhat after June, and the work was even republished—with some modifications—in a collection of Nekrasov's travel notes entitled *Travels in Various Dimensions.*[3] The subjective nature of Nekrasov's travel memoirs is reflected in the very title of the collection which is further elaborated upon by the author in his preface:

> There is another type of travel, no less interesting—travel through time. No, not in search of Calibans or for the Knights of King Arthur (which, by the way, is just as interesting), but in search of something that is dear to oneself, indispensable, but

alas, nowhere near. Could it be a search for oneself, a journey through one's own life? It is difficult
for me to explain this now. I hope that the reader
will understand what I mean as he reads this book.
So let's hit the road for an unusual journey through
time and space.

Nekrasov's "search for oneself" is strongly reminiscent
of Voznesensky's "discovery of myself in myself."

The move away from the travel diary or itinerary
format of the travel memoir toward a more loosely structured, informal approach is further underscored by some
of Nekrasov's comments in the essay on Italy where he
talks about his disdain for travel notes in general:

> . . . in my opinion, a writer needs a notebook only
> to carry addresses and telephone numbers. For any-
> thing else, it just gets in the way. The magic of notes,
> their selectivity, so to speak, usually destroys the
> spontaneity of remembrance. It can be compared
> to the frequent retelling of the same story, which
> soon disintegrates into small talk. The story turns
> into a polished, rehearsed performance. Certain de-
> tails, tested by public exposure, become fixed in
> place, yielding no room to others.
> I don't know how others feel, but I am against
> notebooks.[4]
> . . . . .
> In a word, I promise no order ahead.[5]

Indeed, Nekrasov's "unusual journey through time
and space" does not follow a chronological or spatial plan.
Like Voznesensky's poems, Nekrasov's paragraphs arrange themselves arbitrarily, "outside theme or geography."

Such arbitrary arrangement of subject matter allows the author to expound at will on his thoughts and impressions. He is free of facts, dates, schedules, and whatever else might impose limitations on his needs to express himself. *On Both Sides of the Ocean* contains little concrete description of America. Instead the work is composed mainly of observations which, though related to the trip at hand only indirectly, are full of informal discussions of American life as the author saw it.

There is no cryptography and little ambiguity in Nekrasov's essay on America. The author is quite candid in his commentary as well as in his explanations of what motivated his remaks. However, he seems to have taken pains to disperse some of his more outspoken comments throughout his text, as if to soften their impact. In one instance he speaks in the Italian essay of an incident from his trip to America. He describes the attitude of one of the journalists in his group:

> [This reminds me] of the comment of a not very intelligent journalist with whom I traveled in America. On the third or fourth day he began to complain:
> "When in the world are they going to show us the slums!? So far there's nothing to write about, everything is smooth, clean and comfortable."
> Somehow, I just don't want to emulate him. We saw slums, and terrible unlighted Chicago streets with trains rattling by overhead; we saw the classic unemployed on the Bowery in New York; and even worse—though we didn't go to the South, we watched on television the Negro schoolchildren going to school, guarded by policemen to keep the crowds from tearing them apart. We saw all of this, and it all exists. But is it really worth going to a foreign country if this is all that interests you? Somehow

> I always feel ashamed when people rejoice over others'
> misfortunes. When I see slums, I am sorry for the
> people who live in them, and I am not in the least
> bit glad that these terrible homes and barracks still
> exist—even in a capitalist country. That same jour-
> nalist also said to me:
> "What the devil! Did you see that Negroes are
> living in our hotel? A pair of them even sat in the
> restaurant!"
> It seemed to me that he was actually upset that
> these two Negroes were not forcibly thrown out of
> the restaurant. That would have made a good maga-
> zine article! In the South they actually do throw
> them out, but this doesn't please me in the least.[6]

This passage is an even more outspoken refusal to revel
in the misfortunes of America; it follows the pattern of
humanistic concern first voiced in Voznesensky's poem
"Striptease."

Later, in the American essay, Nekrasov continues
his disparaging report on this same Soviet journalist:

> That same Kievan reporter—we'll call him K.—
> the member of our tourist group who was upset that
> he had nothing to write about because he hadn't seen
> any slums, returned home and straightway began to
> give a series of lectures. Posters appeared all over
> town: "America, November 1960." I went to one of
> these lectures. K. talked in great detail about the
> contrasts, the slums, the unemployed, poverty, the
> sunless streets in New York, the terrible working
> conditions, the high rents of apartments, discrimina-
> tion against the Negroes, strikes—about everything
> that he knew existed before he went to America. He
> didn't say one word about the people. When asked

about the price of goods, he replied that that did not interest him. A whisper ran through the hall. A young man shyly asked about alcoholism in America—was there much drinking there? K. answered: "Quite a lot. In Washington, no, sorry, in Chicago we saw a drunk who could hardly stand on his feet." A roar of laughter raced through the hall. I was ashamed, although I know that one doesn't meet people such as K. everywhere, thank the Lord.[7]

Nekrasov's division of his criticism of this Soviet journalist into two installments, one of which he includes in the essay on Italy, is significant. It might have been too explosive if presented all at once and in its logical context. He further clarifies his own position by reporting the advice of another Soviet journalist who had spent four years in New York:

America is truly a country of contrasts—very striking contrasts. Poverty and wealth, beauty and ugliness exist side by side. But when you speak of contrasts, you must remember to retain a sense of proportion between black and white. I beg you, if you're going to write about America, keep in mind the expression "fifty-fifty," as they say there. Don't write that American youth is interested only in rock-and-roll and baseball. They are interested in these things, and they do enjoy them, but, believe me, they also read the newspapers, and magazines, and books. And they will read your article. Remember this, so you won't have cause to blush.[8]

Nekrasov then goes on to a clear formulation of his own intentions:

I am personally convinced that when telling about the life of some country or other, one cannot, under any circumstances, stick to some percentage norm. The matter does not lie in percentages, but in the ability to see and the attempt to understand what you see, as well as in the thoughts and associations which various events and meetings evoke in you. To pretend to more is difficult when one is writing not a scientific work, but travel notes.[9]

This paragraph originally read:

I personally do not intend to confine myself to any set proportions, and shall try my best to avoid generalities (I just didn't see enough). I shall try to report only what I saw, as well as whatever thoughts and associations were evoked by the events and acquaintances I personally experienced in America. I shall not pretend to more.[10]

The rewriting of this passage, no doubt prompted by the censor as well as the sharp criticism of Nekrasov's "fifty-fifty" approach (see below), has somewhat softened the tone of the statement, but the author still remains firm in his opinion.

Nekrasov's outspoken unorthodoxy created a furor in the Soviet press. An article in *Izvestia* was quite strong in its criticism of Nekrasov for his "extremely superficial and highly erroneous thoughts and associations":

Although he claims to have rejected the advice of a journalist to follow a ratio of "fifty-fifty" when describing America's contrasts, V. Nekrasov has in fact taken this stand. And not only in telling about the black and white aspects of the American way of life. That is only part of the trouble. The real shame is that V. Nekrasov followed this "fifty-fifty" formula in far more serious matters, in comparing the "two worlds," the two ideologies.

Just what does "fifty-fifty" actually mean? If this expression is translated from Aesopian language into ordinary language, we have a motto that proclaims and affirms peaceful coexistence in the field of ideology. "Fifty-fifty" is a very dangerous thing. Following such a formula, willingly or not, it becomes possible to equate the battle on the Volga with American canned pork, Le Corbusier's blueprints with the silhouettes of the cities of the Communist tomorrow. No, we cannot agree to this.

. . . . .

It is completely incomprehensible that a Soviet writer could fail to see the striking social contrasts and class contradictions of American life, or the war psychosis fanned by the imperialist circles. It is difficult for such a tourist, be he superphenomenally observant, to understand the life of a foreign country in a profound way. As a rule, a "façade" acquaintance cannot give an accurate conception about the life of a people, especially of such a large people as the Americans. None the less, V. Nekrasov does not merely share his impressions, but constantly tries to generalize, in the process of which he vilifies what is sacred to every Soviet person. We do not even mention the author's tactless and insulting attitude toward his comrades on the tour.

We repeat, it is not a matter of factual mistakes, but of frivolous and untrue generalizations and parallels which lead to bourgeois objectivism, and of superficial descriptions that distort reality.[11]

There are other specific references to the American trip in the essay on Italy, about one fourth of which is devoted to general observations on travel and travel reportage. Many of these observations are important to the understanding of what Nekrasov wrote about America. Besides such cross references, the Italian and American essays are also similar in style and tone, especially when compared with another essay Nekrasov wrote about his trip to France in December 1962,[12] or with his first travel memoir about Italy, *First Acquaintance*. It is also significant that he traveled as a tourist only in America. In Italy and in France he was representing the Soviet Union at writers' conferences, and so had official meetings to report on as well as his touring. He was more on his own in America, confined by a tighter schedule and a larger group perhaps, but with more scope for observation and the process of association.

The first twenty pages of the essay on Italy are devoted mainly to Nekrasov's thoughts on travel in general. He mentions that he prefers informality. The most pleasant part of a journey is when one ceases to feel like a tourist and becomes a temporary resident who is familiar with the surroundings, indulging in informal conversation with the local people.[13] Nekrasov especially likes heated discussions for getting to the essence of things.[14] And he loves the Italians for their eagerness to take part in the give-and-take of such discussions. Schedules he disdains:

No, not the planned things, not the regimen or notebooks. The most interesting things of all are exactly the opposite—the unexpected: an accidental encounter, a new acquaintance, an on-the-spot argument, an unforeseen question, in other words, things

not in the schedule itself, but in a disruption of the
schedule—my own as well as that of the local inhabitants. More about these disruptions ahead. (They
are concerned not so much with Italy as with the trip
to America, and in general with the organization of
our tourist affairs.) [15]

Nekrasov also makes several comments in the essay
on America deploring the group leader's relentless in-
sistence on keeping to the schedule. This was probably
the more keenly felt because of his tourist status in America
as opposed to his delegate status in Italy and France
where he had been in smaller groups, and, even more
important, among his peers where considerably more freedom had been enjoyed although, ironically, it was needed
less. One of his main complaints in America was the
inflexibility of the group leader, Ivan Ivanovich, who
was always counting the members of the group, lecturing
them, and trying to keep them together. The italicized
sentences in the following excerpt were deleted in the
second edition:

Most of all our dear Ivan Ivanovich feared any
sort of deviation from our daily schedule. He was
constantly counting us, like chickens, and the worst
thing that could happen to him was for someone to
say: "But I don't want to go to the National Gallery,
I want to go to the Guggenheim Museum or perhaps
take a little stroll down Broadway." *For some reason
he especially dreaded this "little stroll."* . . . He gave
us a little speech about discipline, about how so-and-
so had been late for dinner the very first day, and
having separated from the collective had been forced
to take a taxi to catch up. He said this must not

happen again, *otherwise he would be forced to take
the appropriate steps—exactly what, he didn't say.*[16]

The importance of mood and tone in the American
essay can be seen from its unusual beginning:

> I made my first acquaintance with America in
> my native Kiev during the bare and difficult year
> of 1923. I was twelve years old and I used to go
> barefoot (wooden clogs and rope-soled shoes were
> an unobtainable luxury) to the fifth grade of Labor
> School 43.
> America (or as we used to call it in those days,
> the United States of Northern America)—I knew it
> mainly from Mayne Reed and Cooper, from the post-
> age stamps (which were not very interesting, being
> mostly Presidents' pictures), and also from the con-
> densed milk which Hoover's American Relief Ad-
> ministration fed us children (we also eagerly collected
> the buffalo and Indian pictures on the can labels).
> In addition, I used to stop on the way to school to
> read the copies of *Proletarskaya Pravda* pasted on
> the walls, and try to make out the news (it was printed
> on blue wrapping paper) about the Greco-Turkish
> War and the Washington Conference. I had not yet
> seen any American films. That came the following
> year with "The Empress of the World," "The Queen
> of the Forest," and "The Jungle Goddess." But I had
> never set eyes on a live American. The milk and the
> snow-white rolls, soft as cotton, were given out at
> the ARA by Russians.[17]

The America presented here is the America that so
captured the imagination of the Russian people in the
early part of the century: the semiexotic land of the stories

of Mayne Reed and James Fenimore Cooper. The open acknowledgement of American aid to Russia during the famine-ridden years after the Civil War is quite rare for Soviet literature.[18] Nekrasov continues with a description of his first personal acquaintance with an American:

> And then one fine day in Kiev a guest arrived to stay with us (there were no hotels in town, and my aunt worked in the library of the Academy of Sciences). He was none other than the Director of the New York Public Library, Mr. Harry Miller Lydenberg, a lean, middle-aged man. Slung from his shoulder by a small strap was a portable typewriter on which he used to peck out long letters home every day. A little bell rang at the end of each line that sent me running to see who was at the door at first.[19]

A positive and personal tone is set by this opening— a passage that has nothing to do with the writer's trip to America. However, an author's first paragraphs are never accidental. Nekrasov's first impressions of America were not of a land of insensitive, exploiting capitalists, but of a land of generosity toward less fortunate nations, a land whose first ambassadors were librarians and technicians. Apparently the author wants to remind his Soviet readers of these things. Mr. Lydenberg is described as a gentle man, unspoiled and undemanding. After dinner he offered to help with the dishes, as he usually did at home. And though his hosts had carefully prepared a bath for him—a major undertaking in those difficult days —he did not use it. The following morning, he left a coin on his pillow for them. Nekrasov reports that his family was a bit offended by this gesture, but also deeply moved by it. He concludes:

And that is all that I remember about Harry Miller
Lydenberg, the Director of one of the largest libraries
in the world, the first American I ever met. *I liked
him.*[20]

The italicized sentence was deleted in the second edition.
This is significant because it serves to tone down Nekrasov's positive feeling toward America, especially since the
next paragraph, describing his second American acquaintance, a building technician, ends with the words: "I
didn't like this American very much; he was rather a
bore"—and these were not deleted.

Since Mr. Lydenberg's portrait is presented through
the eyes of a child, the honest impression of a good man
is strengthened. First impressions are important whether
in life or in art; so it is significant that the author chose
to begin his essay on America with an affectionate description of his first impression of an American. This introduction reinforces the personal nature of the essay as
well, and seems to stress the importance of personal impressions in life, especially the life of the writer.

Nekrasov continues with a description of the second
American he knew, a technician who assisted in the construction of the Kiev railroad station. His name was Mr.
Borkgravink. Nekrasov describes him as a man who patiently stood his turn in the food line with the other
workers and wrote numerous long memoranda. This
American seemed a bit dull to the author, and as mentioned above, he did not like him very much. But his
lack of affection for the man is based on the latter's color-
less personality and does not interfere with a respect for
his technological knowledge or his hard work. Unlike the
current propagandist techniques, Nekrasov's description
does not turn Mr. Borkgravink into a caricature. He

merely points out that people are different individuals, and should be judged each man for himself. Both Lydenberg and Borkgravink are briefly but realistically presented. In a more recently published memoir, Nekrasov describes a visit by Lydenberg's grandson, Steve, who came to see him in Kiev in 1966. Excerpts from the grandfather's letters (which Nekrasov received from the family after his essay on America was published), describing Soviet life in 1923, are incorporated into the text, as are some of the grandson's comments on travel in the Soviet Union.[21] Nekrasov, thus, seems to be continuing his emphasis on personal relationships and the "great power of friendship," as well as the need for honest exchange and attempts at understanding between America and the Soviet Union, despite the official attacks on his conciliatory tone.

The ability to sketch a character in a few brief lines is one of Nekrasov's strongest talents as a writer: one or two personal features, a gesture or two, an action or two, and the character stands vividly before us. He is also very good at subtle reminders of more amiable relations between America and the Soviet Union in the past. Besides the mention of the American Relief Administration and the technological assistance during the thirties, Nekrasov recalls the alliance of World War II when he met his "third American," a Sherman tank in which he rode to the front. Later in the essay, he makes another specific reference to the assistance America rendered the Soviet Union during the War:

. . . a Russian knows how to value friendship, and we shall never forget the contribution of the Americans who organized various committees to aid the Soviet Union, who collected food, medicine and warm clothing, and who died while trying to get these things to our shores.[22]

This passage originally read:

> We are hardly inclined to minimize our efforts during the war, but nevertheless, we Russians shall never forget the assistance extended to us in those difficult days: the Sherman tanks, the Aero-Cobras, the Studebakers, the canned pork, and all the things which we did not see at the front but which were given to our industries.[23]

This is one of the passages specifically mentioned in the *Izvestia* article quoted above. The rewriting shifts the emphasis from governmental military assistance to personal charity.

Thus, the first two pages set a very positive, relaxed, and informal tone for the writer's exposition of his impressions from his first actual visit to America. This tone, echoing Voznesensky's personalized approach, continues throughout the essay. Nekrasov begins the trip itself with a brief résumé of the flight from Moscow:

> A good many years went by. And then, in the fall of 1960, or more precisely, on the second of November, at 9:30 P.M. New York time, I first landed on American soil, or rather concrete, at Idlewild International Airport.
>
> Say what you will, it is incomprehensible that one can get halfway around the globe in one day. In the morning we were in frosty, snowy Moscow. Twelve hours later we were carrying our coats in our arms in New York City.[24]

This passage offers a good example of Nekrasov's drawn-out, almost conversational tone in his writing. It also shows his eye for detail and his deliberate exposition. After a few more words about the plane trip, he returns to his theme of personal exploration, unequivocally disassociating himself from the subject matter of propaganda:

> I foresee a thousand questions: Is it true that the Ku Klux Klan terrorizes everybody? Is it true that a crime is committed every six minutes in New York? That the summer temperature reaches 110° in the shade? That every American owns one fourth of an automobile? *And 995 other questions. I simply am not able to answer them all. I shall try to relate what I saw with my own eyes.* And I shall avoid statistics wherever I can, even though the Americans are very fond of them—perhaps for this very reason.[25]

The italicized lines appeared in a more resolute form in the journal version:

> That—No! I shall not answer a single such question. I shall talk only about what I saw with my own eyes.[26]

The revised text somewhat modifies the determined tone of the original. The difference between "I shall not" and "I am not able to" is subtle, but significant. The changes delete Nekrasov's emphatic point that it is a certain type of question he abhors. Such textual alterations reveal the Party's concern about objectivity toward America, and the censor's attempts to tone it down when it does appear.

Before he gets down to reporting his impressions of America, Nekrasov makes yet another digression to describe his group:

> I shall begin with New York—no, with our group. We are not a delegation, we are tourists. There are twenty of us: teachers, journalists, engineers—members of the so-called Soviet intelligentsia.[27]

The group members are not identified further—unlike the more usual Soviet tourist who is careful to give full particulars on the illustrious members of the delegation. Nekrasov again reinforces the personal nature of his travel notes—he does not talk of group activity (except disparagingly). He assumes the role of narrator, not of reporter.

The itinerary is given: New York, Washington, Chicago, Niagara, Detroit, Dearborn and Buffalo. It is not mentioned again. Nekrasov discusses only those places that especially interested him. More important, he launches into frequent digressions on topics close to his heart, topics that usually lie beyond the narrow confines of socialist-realism. Besides beating Emily Post to the writing of a pamphlet on etiquette for the Soviet tourist, he discusses subjects such as art, international relations, and propaganda, stating his firm disagreement with Soviet policies in many cases.

Nekrasov is quite candid about the difficulty of getting to know a foreign country, especially one that is considered alien in respects other than geographical:

> America is a special country. One of our writers who visited America said: "What surprised me most

about America was the fact that nothing surprised me." Somehow this is hard to believe. At any rate I was surprised by a great deal, even though I was prepared for much of what I saw: the skyscrapers, the abundance of automobiles, the lights on Broadway, the Sunday newspaper that weighs over two pounds. But it is these very things: the gigantic homes, the gigantic cities, the highways cutting across the entire country with millions of automobiles on them, the twenty-story department stores, the endless bacchanalia of advertising, the famous American service—in a word, all this external wealth and abundance that overwhelms you immediately, but at the same time interferes with a deeper and more fundamental understanding of things.

In order even to begin to penetrate into the essence of things, to reach any depth at all, you need to do more than just visit museums, climb to the top of the Empire State Building, or photograph Niagara Falls. You need something far more complicated: the ability to investigate thoroughly everything you see soberly, honestly and without prejudice. But this is not as easy as it seems. *At the present time, we and America, or rather the United States, are not exactly bosom friends. In ideological and political affairs, we are adversaries.*[28]

The italicized sentences were rewritten from a much stronger, a more more significant comment about the Cold War in the earlier version:

That is to say, we are not friendly with America, or rather with the United States. We, the two strongest and most powerful governments in the world, are adversaries in ideological and political relations.

Twenty years ago we were allies, but now we are
adversaries. This is a horrible word. One doesn't
like to use it; maybe it's not necessary. But it doesn't
pay to hide your head under your wing either. We
do not trust one another. We are wary of one another.
We accuse one another.[29]

After explaining his approach to America and giving
a very brief but comprehensive description of its material
wealth, and also speaking quite candidly about the contemporary state of Soviet-American relations, Nekrasov
continues with a paragraph that reemphasizes his concern with getting to know the people of a foreign land
despite the obstacles:

Under these conditions it is not easy to travel
around the country, much less write about it. Nor
is it a simple matter to communicate with the people.
And communication, whether with friends or with
enemies, is the most important thing. Only through
communication can you get through to what interests
you in any depth at all. Life and what people live
by are the most interesting things of all. Then come
the Empire State and the Chrysler Buildings.[30]

As he is critical of the reports of some Soviet journalists about America, so he voices his displeasure over
the behavior of some Soviet tourists in America. He compares two members of his group in another digression:

I remember the dark anguish one of our tourists
(a university professor) caused our hospitable hosts
and their guests in Buffalo when, after the second
glass of cognac, he pulled out his notebook and

began a long recital of statistics on the production
of steel, pig iron, manganese and coal in the Ukraine.
I also remember how, on the other hand, everyone
was enchanted with another one of our tourists (a
young Moscow journalist), who conquered everyone
with the first words he addressed to the host:
"I see you have the latest model Ford in your
garage. May I take it out for a spin at 100 miles an
hour?"
He took his spin, and examined the motor with
the owner, and argued about the latest baseball games,
and challenged someone to a wrestling match—and
the Americans couldn't tear themselves away from
him. But our poor professor sat in the corner with
his statistics in his pocket, forgotten by all.
Yes, be yourself first of all, and then a preacher.
By the way, isn't that the best sermon—being yourself?[31]

Such digressions in the beginning of Nekrasov's
essay on America are numerous and important, and he
has written them carefully. They help to set a definite
mood (friendly) and define the purpose of his travels
(open-minded inquiry into American life). He often compares the Soviet with the American aspects of a given
situation or subject. In many ways he is kinder to America
than he is to the Soviet Union. In general, he shies away
from criticizing the United States on the usual subjects
that Communist propaganda so delights in exposing:
slums, exploitation, poverty, racism. But he does not
hesitate to say what he does not like about Soviet life.
Nekrasov finds much that he likes in America, and
he says so—openly and in great detail. As an architect
himself, he devotes special attention to American architecture, which he admires: "The art of America is archi-

tecture. Or to be more accurate—her genius for construction."[32] He is delighted by the American skyscrapers:

> Reports that they are depressing are mistaken. Many
> of them, those built in recent years, are very light
> (yes, light!), airy, transparent. There is a great deal
> of glass in them, and they reflect each other in a
> very amusing way. In the morning and evening, when
> the sun strikes them at an angle and lights them up,
> they are simply beautiful.[33]

Unlike many Soviet visitors who find American skyscrapers depressing and unaesthetic, Nekrasov considers them to be a "perfected functional-aesthetic form"—especially the Seagram Building and Lever House, which he cites as "crowning examples" of these "glass and steel parallelepipeds."[34] Nekrasov's views on skyscrapers have apparently changed somewhat since his first trip abroad in 1957. In "First Acquaintance" he describes a Milan skyscraper as a "fright" [*strašilišče*], commenting further: "In the capitalist world lots are bought and sold, and if you buy one, you may build whatever suits your fancy, spitting from the heights of the thirtieth floor on all the palaces and castles around you."[35] This sarcastic tone is noticeably absent in *On Both Sides of the Ocean*.

The two mammoth cities, New York and Chicago, enchanted him. Here are two very similar impressionistic descriptions of these two American cities:

> Once, very early in the morning, I walked along
> the streets in the dock area by the Hudson. The end-
> less fences of the warehouses stretched out with their
> enormous billboards, somewhere in the distance

switch engines were whistling just the way ours do, and tattered cats were snooping around and scampering across the street. Suddenly, as I turned up a side street, I saw the Empire State Building. It was still blanketed in morning mist, but the very uppermost stories were already turning rosy from the sun. Its windows were gleaming, and all around it were other enormous shapes, only slightly smaller, waiting for the sun to reach them. Down below in the canyons it was chilly. The predawn twilight had not yet dissolved. That very morning I understood the beauty of that enormous, contradictory city—the beauty of its glass and steel, the beauty of its architecture.[36]

. . . . .

A friend and I wandered along the shore of Lake Michigan in Chicago. The night before it had been snowing and raining, bathing the city in a fog turned reddish-yellow by the lights from advertising signs. The wet asphalt had glistened. But now the weather had cleared up, the sun was shining, and the lake, as large as a sea, was quietly rolling its flat waves over the wide, deserted, cold beach. All around it was surprisingly, improbably empty. Automobiles were sweeping by—low, wide, noiseless; but no people were around. We were alone on the endless lakefront. There was nothing for a Chicagoan to do there; it wasn't summer and the beach was closed. (And what a beach! We should have one like it at Yalta.) The deserted landscape, the absence of human beings, the almost idyllic stillness gave us the chance to see the city—the most American of all the cities; even more American than New York—to see it from the sidelines, without haste, without hurrying to get somewhere, sitting on the parapet, smoking a cigarette, lazily conversing. . . . Beautiful! By God, beautiful. What a city![37]

Perhaps to balance his report on Chicago, he notes on the following page that it is a great city for Soviets because the American Communist Party was born there. But there can be no doubt as to his genuine admiration for the city from an architectural point of view, as well as for the beauty of the lakefront. His remark about Yalta is a most unusual concession in print.

As Chicago is the "most American" city for Nekrasov, Washington, D.C. is the "least American" city—because of its provincial nature:

> Washington is the least American of all American cities. There is almost no industry, the streets are wide and green, the houses are low. It is a quiet, peaceful city of government officials which retires early.[38]

The view from the top of the Empire State Building overwhelmed Nekrasov:

> I must say, that when you stand above this city and somewhere below you dozens of skyscrapers are clustered together in the enormous horizon while little creatures and tiny automobiles crawl among them in the canyons below; and beyond you lies the East River and the Brooklyn Bridge, and the Hudson with its docks and ships—when you stand up there with the wind in your face, and look down at this giant city, or octopus-city—call it what you will—you can't help but feel excited. I once experienced a similar feeling on the peak of Mount Elbrus. The Caucasus at my feet! Everything lay below me. Even Mount Kazbek was beneath me. But there I was struck by the grandeur and beauty of nature. Here I was struck

by the grandeur and beauty of man's labor. For he
made it all—his hands and his brain.[39]

The comparison with the Caucasus is interesting.
Nekrasov seems to share Mayakovsky's great enthusiasm
for the creative structures of man, as voiced in the latter's
poem, "Brooklyn Bridge." The few lines following the
above passage reflect Nekrasov's grave concern for the
direction of man's building:

> And then you have to ask yourself a question: How
> many Empire State and Chrysler Buildings, and
> bridges like the swift and airy George Washington
> Bridge across the Hudson, how many useful things
> could be built with the money that is being spent on
> all the Polarises, Honest Johns, and other merry
> playthings of the twentieth century?

Nekrasov also reports favorably on a few pet targets
of Soviet propaganda—he enjoyed an Elvis Presley movie[40]
and found Coca-Cola to be a refreshing drink: "We've
made fun of it for no good reason. It's a delicious and
really refreshing drink." [41] And he was unable to resist
an Anacin commercial:

> And imagine, the advertising really works! It even
> worked on us. We finally all went out and bought
> some magic Anacin tablets to relieve headaches—
> even I, who never suffer from this ailment.[42]

Besides architecture, Nekrasov devotes a great deal
of space to art and to films in his travel notes on America.
Particularly telling is his discussion of Soviet films and

his defense of the new liberal trend of some Soviet film directors. He is also receptive to some of the modern art in America, and shares Voznesensky's enthusiasm for the Guggenheim Museum:

> We often like to compare unusual objects with familiar ones. The Schusev Theater in Rostov, for example, was considered to resemble a tractor. Something else there, I forget what, looked like an airplane. The Guggenheim Museum doesn't resemble anything (although some of our tourists said that it reminded them of a ship; others, of a washing machine). It is an enormous white spiral of reinforced concrete that widens towards the top and is attached to a broad horizontal base. The rest of the dimensions complement and emphasize the basic ones. The enormous spiral is the museum itself. You go up in an elevator to the very top, and then you descend around the spiral, which is actually a gallery with an inner courtyard. The spiral is 4000 feet long. I have never in my life seen a museum arranged more rationally, or more conveniently— for both the viewer and for the displays. The pictures hang in a single row, at eye level. To be exact, they do not hang, but are fastened to the wall with brackets, creating the illusion that they soar in space against the white walls. There is a lot of air, a lot of light (both natural and artificial—the two being blended very successfully), a lot of greenery, and even a pool with a little fountain.
>
> The museum's collection is rich and varied: Cezanne, Modigliani, Leger, Picasso, Paul Klee, Kandinsky, Chagall, sculptures by Lipshitz and Brancusi —in short, all the most interesting artists the West has produced since the end of the nineteenth century. And I must say that the fusion between the archi-

tecture and the exhibited works of art is perfect.
The pictures and sculptures are in a comfortable
and spacious setting. They are at home.[43]

It is interesting to compare the above with Nekrasov's first recorded impression of modern art in his essay
First Acquaintance:

> I have no doubt that even "abstract" art has a right
> to its place under the sun. But not, of course, in a
> museum where it is presented as a painting that pre-
> tends to some sort of higher content.[44]

On this trip he is rather more receptive to such art, being
intrigued even by an abstract mobile in the airport
terminal:

> From the ceiling of the lobby hangs a slowly revolving
> sort of many-headed construction that considers itself
> a sculpture. (Incidently, the thing in itself was very
> appealing to me. It had a pterodactyl-helicopter qual-
> ity about it—in other words: aviation.) [45]

Nekrasov also devotes a few pages to the surrealist
painter, Salvador Dali:

> Dali is an artist endowed with a cultivated imagina-
> tion and is a superb draftsman. Looking at his paint-
> ings you see *how much work* has gone into them.
> This is no mish-mash.[46]

The italicized words read "how much great and difficult
work" in the first version. The end of the paragraph had

an additional phrase as well: "This is work." The deletions serve to de-emphasize Dali's stature as an artist, as
does the excision of the words "most talented" a few
lines above this passage. This is, of course, consistent
with the Party's taboo against surrealism in art.

The author goes on to introduce a slight disagreement with no less an authority than the Soviet encyclopedia:

> If we are to believe the *Large Soviet Encyclopedia*
> (*cf.* the article on "Surrealism," volume 41): "The
> well-known representative of surrealism, the painter
> Salvador Dali, paints pictures that glorify atomic
> war."—This is put briefly and expressively, but un-
> fortunately it does not quite correspond to the truth.
> Dali, of course, does not glorify any sort of war. He
> does not glorify or condemn anything at all. Salvador
> Dali, like surrealism itself, is a much more complex
> phenomenon, even if it is completely consistent *for
> bourgeois art, in the manifestation of its deteriora-
> tion.*[47]

A somewhat less didactic phrase, "with the development
of Western art," stands in place of the italicized words
in the original.

Nekrasov also uses Dali as a launching pad to voice
a negative opinion on Soviet art:

> Dali fled from realism to the dream, to the nightmare,
> to surrealism. Some of our painters seem to be run-
> ning just as hard in the opposite direction, toward
> a studiously flattened, triumphantly saccharine sort
> of antireality, of antirealism.[48]

Earlier in the essay, Nekrasov talks about imagery, during the course of which he is quite sharp in his criticism of Soviet art: (italicized sentence deleted from second edition):

> Imagery—How often we talk about it and how often we forget that art can not exist without it. Dead and living water. Dead water can only stick the broken body together; living water pours life, a soul into it. . . . A true work of art, a great work, is living water.
> Living and dead water—*How many years they've been giving us dead water.*[49]

In two pages added to the new edition of his essay on America, Nekrasov writes quite enthusiastically about the paintings of Grandma Moses, which he did not see until a Moscow exhibit in 1964:

> Grandma Moses' pictures are short stories: very detailed, unhurried and thorough. Her entire life is portrayed in them: childhood, youth, maturity, old age. They show the farm where she spent almost her entire life: the hills, the woods, the streams, the old windmill. In winter, summer, autumn and spring. The minor as well as the major events of her life. The Turkey Hunt Before Christmas—that's what the picture is named. Wedding. Christmas Night. Grandma Goes to New York—it's impossible to tear oneself away from this last picture.[50]

There are few things that Nekrasov criticizes about America in his travel notes. He keeps to his word that he will steer clear of the usual anti-American topics and concentrate on his personal impressions. His strongest statements are about what he considers the appalling state of American television (too much violence) and the vast amount of detective fiction which the youth are reading instead of Faulkner:

> Yes, American television is something horrible. I had heard a lot about it, but I had to see it to understand. Really, how can you avoid killing your neighbor, how can you help dealing him a good "knockout" punch, when from morning until night the television shows you the best ways to do it. And if you don't do it yourself, others will do it to you.[51]
>
> . . . . .
>
> The second scourge of America is the broad, dark stream of detective literature. It is literally a sea overflowing. So much has already been written on the subject—about all the covers with pistols pointing at you—that I'm almost ashamed to write any more. But I cannot remain silent. I do not want to say anything derogatory about American bookstores—there are a lot of good, interesting, serious books. But good books are expensive, while all this detective poison costs pennies and gets into you before you realize it. The worst part is that they avidly swallow it. Especially the young.[52]

Even Nekrasov's criticisms of America are noticeable for the absence of self-righteousness. His main concern is for the welfare of the Americans who indulge in these entertainments. He does not engage in irrational criticism as propagandists are inclined to do. He follows the rational and humanistic approach first noted in Voznesensky.

In fact, he even proceeds to criticize the boring content
of Soviet television:

> By the way, to speak seriously, television is the
> scourge not only of America. We don't have fighting
> or brawling or wrestling on our television, but we
> have something else: we bore our audiences to death
> with endless interviews and repetitive amateur hours
> that resemble each other like drops of water.[53]

Like most Soviet visitors to America, Nekrasov reports meeting some Russian emigrants who are very unhappy in America and long to return to the motherland.
He meets a Ukrainian at Niagara Falls who is so over-
joyed to hear Russian being spoken and to smoke a Russian cigarette that he cannot bear to leave the group. It
seems he is not happy with his work in America and
is quite homesick for Kiev.[54] This meeting reminds the
author of his encounter the week before in New York
with a woman he knew before the war. She, too, is very
lonely and unhappy—her son and granddaughter are in
the Soviet Union. Nekrasov comments: "The Russian
abroad. The Ukrainian abroad. Most of these cases are
tragedies."[55] He relates a third sad emigrant story about
a daughter of friends of his in Kiev who is lonely in
Australia. Another emigrant who was their guide in
Brussels, however, seems fairly well settled in his new
life, although he enjoys meeting with Soviet tourists so
much that he serves as a guide gratuitously. The status
of Russian emigrants in America is apparently a topic
of much interest to Soviet readers (or perhaps it is of
interest to the propagandists), as it is written about a
lot in travel reports, and usually bathetically. Nekrasov

devotes six pages to the topic and seems to follow the trend.

About yet another emigrant, one Tadeus Osipovich, the American Express guide for the group, Nekrasov was rather unkind in his travel notes. He describes him as rather brusque and too schedule-conscious, and was irritated by his skipping the Guggenheim Museum as unimportant and, at the end of the trip, accusing the group of dereliction in their gratitude to him by failing to present him with a bottle of vodka. Nekrasov repeats this guide's final speech to the group:

"To be quite frank, I'm not only hurt, but astonished. You are not my first Soviet group. And always, on the day of departure, they give me a bottle of *Stolichnaya*. You know, I don't drink, but I like to go to the office, show the bottle, and say, 'Look how my Soviet tourists expressed their gratitude.' You are the first group who have not brought me any vodka. I am very offended." [56]

Nekrasov then goes on to address the unfortunate Tadeus Osipovich in the text to tell him that the group had planned a special goodbye for him, but his little speech ruined it all. The motivation for the inclusion of this episode in the memoirs is rather puzzling. It is about the only moralizing that Nekrasov allows himself in this work. However, he does seem a bit oversensitive at times, and his chivalric objectivity fades somewhat. He also reports being quite upset when a group of students at Columbia University failed to show up (apparently as a result of poor logistics) and a professor took him to a student lounge where the students "did not find me

interesting enough to talk to." [57] And he sadly notes that
he did not make any new friends during his two weeks
in America. How different from Italy!—where his notebook was soon full of names. In America he made only
two or three casual entries.

The author reports meeting with young Americans
twice besides the unsuccessful occasion with the Columbia
students. A very pleasant encounter with a group of
gregarious high-school boys occurs on the train from
Buffalo. Nekrasov is quite taken with the youngsters
who enjoy practicing their Russian with him, but he
worries about their desire to "go into business" when
they grow older. He is, however, confident that they will
eventually read Faulkner as well. The other encounter
is with a young man named Volodya, the son of Russian
emigrant parents. Nekrasov and Volodya engage in a
long discussion over the relative merits of the American
and the Soviet systems. Nekrasov does not recount much
of the substance of this night-long conversation, but he
does say that the dispute ended with Volodya, much to his
own surprise, admitting defeat. This is about the only
propagandizing that Nekrasov does in the course of his
American travel notes, aside from a somewhat naive
comparison of Soviet and American youth:

> There is such a concept as duty: duty toward one's
> people, toward one's country. I think that's the main
> thing that distinguishes our youth from the youth
> of the bourgeois West.[58]
>
> . . . . .
>
> I don't mean to idealize all our youngsters who
> go out to the construction projects. Not all of them
> are motivated by idealistic reasons, far from it. But
> a good many of them do go because they think they

are helping their country. Is such a thing possible in America? I doubt it. The young American, even the searching and thinking American, is concerned first of all with himself, with his own career. It is hard to imagine one of our young men saying, for example: "I want this because it's to my advantage." This would be considered simply improper. Even if he thought so, he would never utter it aloud; he would simply be ashamed to. The young American, on the other hand, considers this completely normal. It's not his fault. It is demanded by the iron laws of the society in which he lives.[59]

Nekrasov closes his essay with a poignant episode. On his last night in America he takes a subway to Harlem. There he goes into a bar, orders a drink, and starts talking to a young American, Patrick Stanley. Patrick was an aviator during the war, and fought on the same front as did Nekrasov. After a few drinks together, mutual exchanges about their families, and common regrets over the Cold War, they reluctantly say goodbye. The author then tells us that this touching scene is only make-believe:

Patrick Stanley. Flying Fortress. Gunner-radioman. How sorry I am that I did not manage to meet you, that this whole story of my late-night trip, the saloon, the beautiful Negress, the pack of *Belomors,* are all something I invented. There was no bar, no Negress, no Patrick. There was only the wish that there had been. That we sat like that in the little bar and remembered the war, had a few drinks, and wandered about the streets at night. That Jim really existed—a good lad even if he doesn't like school (and there are lads like that). A wish that he would come to Kiev with his father, so we could visit my

friend and sing songs, and walk along in the still of
the Kievan night past Goloseyev Woods, down Red
Army Street, the Kreshchatik, down to the Dnepr,
where, sitting on the slope, we would watch the sun
rise—How I wish that this had been.[60]

Nekrasov thus ends his travel memoir with an ima-
ginatively expressed wish for friendship. The scene exposes Nekrasov the romantic, the idealist. But it also
shows his deep concern for humanity and his distress
over the Cold War between America and the Soviet Union,
a theme he mentions several times during the course of
the essay. His postscript (Patrick Stanley) skillfully returns the narrative to the conciliatory mood of his introduction. Like Voznesensky he puts aside the ideological
struggle of the political world.

Nekrasov's humanitarian tone and his impressionistic
style are what distinguish this work, like Voznesensky's
poems, from the typical Soviet travel reports. Nekrasov
came to America to observe. He was able to isolate what
seemed to him good and to enjoy it, without forgetting
the bad but without harping on it either. The following
brief paragraph seems to typify these qualities:

I may say that as a city-dweller I like the accentuated urbanity of these cities. I like the skyscrapers made of steel and glass that reflects the clouds
drifting across the sky. I like to look up and see their
vertical edges, precise as a mathematical formula. I
like the disorderly commotion of the skyscrapers,
disrupting the regularity of the streets. I'm talking
about the appearance of the city. Not about its
tragedy: the dust, the heat, the crowded conditions,
the stifling gasoline fumes; nor about the haphazard

layout or the purity of the style of its buildings; but about its appearance.[61]

His impressionism here is reflected in his concentration on appearance and in the selection of some of his imagery —the "accentuated urbanism" of the city, the reflection of passing clouds in the glass walls of the skyscrapers, the "mathematically precise" outlines of the buildings, the contrast of the "disorderly commotion" of the skyscrapers with the regularity of the streets. Again with but a few strokes, Nekrasov has effectively captured the magic of the modern American city. He does not overlook its problems, but he concentrates on its positive aspects.

Thus, in an open, honest, and direct approach, mixing impressionism with realism, Nekrasov has further developed Voznesensky's new direction for the Soviet travel genre. *On Both Sides of the Ocean* also differs substantially from his first travel essay, *First Acquaintance,* in tone and approach. The latter shows the hypersensitivity and the defensive attitude of the typical Soviet tourist which are almost completely missing in the former. Nekrasov has seemingly matured from a provincial need for self-praise to a more cosmopolitan capacity for self-criticism.

Nekrasov's "objectivity" and genuineness were not overlooked by the Party. The reactions in the Soviet press show that there was far more concern over his "objective" portrayal of America than over his criticisms of Soviet life. The Italian trip is not mentioned in the censure proceedings; it was the American essay that prompted the storm of disapproval. Also, most of the deletions in the second edition are aimed at toning down this "objectivity."

Nor did these qualities go unheeded by some other

Soviet writers who have since come to America. They
have followed in Nekrasov's foosteps—by reporting the
good and beauty in America, and by including some
rather sharp criticisms of the Soviet Union in their American travel notes. However, they have not been so candid
in their commentary. Nekrasov resorted to a digressionary
form—his comments on certain sensitive subjects are
carefully dispersed throughout his text. But his language
is simple and direct. Other writers since have taken
greater pains to conceal their true thoughts. One of them,
Valentin Kataev, merits special attention.

Notes

1. V. Nekrasov, *Po obe storony okeana, Novyj mir*, XI, XII
   (November, December 1962).
2. V. Nekrasov, *Pervoe znakomstvo, Novyj mir*, VII, VIII (July,
   August 1958).
3. V. Nekrasov, *Putešestvija v raznyx izmerenijax* (Moscow 1967).
4. *Ibid.*, 10.
5. *Ibid.*, 25.
6. *Ibid.*, 62–63.
7. *Ibid.*, 127–128.
8. *Ibid.*, 128.
9. *Ibid.*, 130.
10. V. Nekrasov, *Novyj mir*, XII (December 1962), 129.
11. "*Turist s trostočkoj,*" *Izvestia*, January 20, 1963, 5.
12. V. Nekrasov, *Mesjac vo Francii, Novyj mir*, IV (April 1965).
13. V. Nekrasov, *Putešestvija*, 18.
14. *Ibid.*, 13.
15. *Ibid.*, 9.
16. *Ibid.*, 90–91.
17. *Ibid.*, 85–86.
18. Frederick C. Barghoorn in *The Soviet Image of the United
    States* (New York 1950) reports that only two American engi-
    neers appeared in Soviet plays covering the period 1926 to
    1941, as Soviet propaganda characteristically played down the
    Soviet debt to Western industrial civilization during this period

(pp. 34–35) and minimized World War II Lend Lease programs
as well (pp. 55–58).

19. V. Nekrasov, *Putešestvija*, 86.
20. *Ibid.*
21. V. Nekrasov, "*Deduška i vnuček*," *Novyj mir*, IX (September 1968).
22. V. Nekrasov, *Putešestvija*, 126.
23. V. Nekrasov, *Novyj mir*, XII (December 1962), 128.
24. V. Nekrasov, *Putešestvija*, 87.
25. *Ibid.*, 88.
26. V. Nekrasov, *Novyj mir*, XII (December 1962), 111.
27. V. Nekrasov, *Putešestvija*, 88.
28. *Ibid.*, 89–90.
29. V. Nekrasov, *Novyj mir*, XII (December 1962), 112.
30. V. Nekrasov, *Putešestvija*, 90.
31. *Ibid.*, 106–107.
32. *Ibid.*, 144.
33. *Ibid.*, 91–92.
34. *Ibid.*, 155.
35. V. Nekrasov, *Novyj mir*, VIII (August 1958), 149.
36. V. Nekrasov, *Putešestvija*, 154–155.
37. *Ibid.*, 151.
38. *Ibid.*, 117.
39. *Ibid.*, 92.
40. *Ibid.*, 97.
41. *Ibid.*, 152.
42. *Ibid.*, 98.
43. *Ibid.*, 157–158. (The spiral is actually only 1400 feet in length.)
44. V. Nekrasov, *Novyj mir*, VII (July 1958), 162.
45. V. Nekrasov, *Putešestvija*, 134.
46. *Ibid.*, 138.
47. *Ibid.*, 139.
48. *Ibid.*, 141.
49. *Ibid.*, 135–136.
50. *Ibid.*, 143.
51. *Ibid.*, 98.
52. *Ibid.*, 99–100.
53. *Ibid.*, 99.
54. *Ibid.*, 165–166.
55. *Ibid.*, 166.
56. *Ibid.*, 120.
57. *Ibid.*, 131.
58. *Ibid.*, 103.
59. *Ibid.*, 105.
60. *Ibid.*, 181.
61. *Ibid.*, 153.

4.

Confrontation: Valentin Kataev,
The Sacred Well

Valentin Kataev, born in 1897, is one of the older generation of Soviet writers who began publishing their works before the revolution or during the early twenties, and who have continued to publish through the times of confusion, repression, and the "Thaw" into the 1960's. With the recent death of his contemporaries, Konstantin Paustovsky and Ilya Ehrenburg, Kataev remains one of the very few living members of this older group. Both he and his younger brother, the late Evgeny Petrov, belong to a circle of writers from the southern seaport town of Odessa who were noted for their ornamental prose.[1]

During the thirties Kataev wrote solid socialist-realism works, and his *Time, Forward!* (1932) is a typical industrial novel of that time. In 1936 he wrote a somewhat more interesting novel, *Lonely White Sail,* about the Odessa workers' revolution of 1905. This work was to become the first part of a socialist-realist tetralogy about the great revolution, published in 1961 under the title, *Waves of the Black Sea.* Kataev is commended in the most recent edition of the Soviet literary encyclopedia as a master of socialist realism: "In his best works Kataev resolves the lofty aims of socialist realism: Communist ideology and profound realism are combined in these works with great artistic mastery." [2]

Suddenly in 1966, at the age of 69, a completely new Kataev emerged on the Soviet literary scene with the appearance of a surrealistic and certainly very unsocialist-realist story, *The Sacred Well*.[3] A central theme of the work is the author's visit to America, fictionalized as a dream of the narrator. The style, themes, and content of this work aroused great interest behind the Iron Curtain as well as in the West. The May 1966 issue of the liberal journal *Novyj mir*, in which the story was to appear, was delayed for a couple of months while discussions, debates, and deletions were undertaken. It finally appeared with minor, though significant alterations,[4] and the critical comment is still pouring in on the work.

Valentin Kataev visited America in the summer of 1959 for two weeks, and again during the winter and spring of 1963 for three months. He did not publish any travel notes on his trips. Possibly influenced by the strong negative reaction of officials to Nekrasov's travel memoirs on America (which came at the very time that Kataev was in America), he chose instead to present his impressions in the form of a fictionalized narrative. *The Sacred Well* recounts a series of dreams under anaesthesia during a major surgical operation. The dreams are a general remembrance of things past, a recalling of several significant experiences of the narrator's lifetime—almost as a drowning man's entire life flashes before his eyes. This is not meant to suggest an analogy with drowning although water imagery does play a significant role in this work. The well may be interpreted here as a symbol of the narrator's inner (sacred) self, thus continuing the deep subjectivism of Voznesensky and Nekrasov. It is fascinating that the voyages of these three writers to America become symbolic expositions of the authors' "voyages" into their own psyches as well. The outer form, or dream-memories, of *The Sacred Well* camouflages a subtle subtext of cryptographic inner themes that run throughout the work. A drug-induced motivation suspends the bounds of ordinary time and space, allowing the narrator to range the widest possible compass of events and sequences with great imagination and, at times, effective surrealism. It also permits him to delve into highly personal experiences and feelings with the claim that he has no conscious control over the wanderings of his unconscious mind. Thus the author ingeniously devises a camouflage for his discovery of America, and of himself.

The larger part of the work, about two thirds, is devoted to the narrator's trip to America. The first part of the story is a series of flashbacks into the narrator's life in the Soviet Union and concerns his family and friends. The flashbacks are "memories" he recalls from a paradisaical plane (an afterlife) which he enters in his state of unconsciousness both before and during surgery.

As the work opens we find the narrator in paradise, living in ideal retirement, from which dimension he goes back in time to his experiences on earth. This double time inversion is a unique device, employed by Kataev to at least partially disguise the highly subjective and un-socialist-realist nature of the work. In some ways the first part of the story acts as a prologue to the American trip—several images and ideas that occur in the American dream have their genesis there, and a few comments about Soviet life are further developed in the dream about America. As is common in cryptographical writing, the most important thoughts of the narrator are scattered fragmentarily through the work, forming a sort of surrealistic mosaic, far more ambiguous and disguised than the "digressions" we noted in Nekrasov's *On Both Sides of the Ocean,* yet not quite as artistically superimposed as in some of Yevtushenko's poems on America which will be discussed in Chapter Five.

As the work begins the narrator has just been given something to make him sleep in preparation for his operation the next morning:

> "I promise you paradisaical dreams."
> "In color?"
> "Any kind you wish," she said and left the ward.

Then begins a truly "paradisaical" dream. The narrator and his wife are in the Soviet version of heaven: their retirement home in Peredelkino, the writers' colony outside of Moscow. *The Sacred Well* is the name of a well near the railroad station, where a mysterious old man comes to wash his seemingly endless collection of bottles:

> . . . and yet the number of bottles in the sack did not diminish, as if the sack were magic. This bothered us a little, like a simple trick that is hard to solve.

The scene shifts dream-like to "Kunmin, city of eternal spring" in Southern China, where another old man with a long beard and mustache offers to sell the narrator and his wife a nasturtium-colored goldfish, and where the first old man continues to wash his bottles. This surrealistic blending of different settings is a dominant feature of the work, and contributes to its ambiguity.

The dream is interrupted by the doctor, who comes in to check his patient before the morning's operation: "I liked his narrow, almost boyish face and his dark, gentle hypnotist's eyes that looked at me penetratingly, as if through the slits of a mask." [5] The vision of the doctor's eyes, slit-like above his mask, reappears several times in the text, in descriptions of other people as "slit-eyed." This may be an attempt to blend the two planes—reality (the operation) and imagination (the dreams)—by recalling from time to time the image of the surgeon at work over his patient. There are several direct references also to the operation itself. However, the two levels of dream and reality are not smoothly interwoven. Although these interruptions disrupt the narrative, the dream itself usually continues as before. They are not inseparable from the dream, as in the stream-of-consciousness writings of James Joyce, or even the fantasies of Gogol, but are rather a sharp contrast to it. Their thematic or symbolic significance, if any, is thus unclear. Their surrealistic nature, however, seems to suggest that they may be chiefly a literary device, a justification to the censor to "rationalize" the "irrationality" of the thought processes here. Also, the dreams themselves are more structured and controlled than the spontaneous associations of the mind in a stream-of-consciousness narrative should be. Many of these episodes are ambiguous and elusive, and are conveyed in a highly impressionistic or even surrealistic style. Interspersed among them are other episodes and comments that are sharply realistic and unambiguous, strongly suggesting that the surrealism is cryptographical in nature.

For example, the narrator's description of life in paradise is quite realistic, portrayed in materialistic terms of physical comfort:

> At first we weren't bored at all. We loved each other again, but now this love was like a mirror image of our previous earthly love. It was quiet and passionless.
>
> . . . . .
>
> Next to the house, as befits dreams in color, there were a few bushes of cultivated lilac with remarkably rich, full and beautiful flowers. We never tired of admiring the different shades of their color.
>
> . . . . .
>
> Nobody bothered us. We lived in fullest satisfaction, each according to his inclinations. I, for instance, taking advantage of my retirement age, tried to do nothing at all. . . . We feasted on large, sweet and always fresh strawberries with sugar and cream, and at sundown we liked to drink a cup of very strong, almost black tea with sugar and a drop of milk.[6]

This passage in many ways recalls the mood and bucolic setting of Gogol's domestic idyll, "Old World Landowners." Kataev's narrator, surrounded by material plenty (nice weather, abundant food, beautiful flowers, and perfect health), can now spend his time in "idle" reflection:

> . . . I tried to do nothing. Not even to think. I just looked out of the window and gathered random observations of no special value, neither scientific, nor artistic, nor philosophical. Thus, for instance, I

noticed that two completely different plants can grow out of the same soil, almost out of the very same spot, one of them beautiful and precious such as a horse chestnut tree, and the other homely and cheap, its wood of poor quality, such as an alder tree. On the whole I paid a lot of attention to matter in one form or another. I came to the conclusion that it is not only content that determines form but something else as well. Observing nature, I concluded that since all we ever see are physical bodies which, as such, possess volume—whether the body of a road, the body of a maple leaf, the numerous little bodies of sand (for each grain of sand is a body), or even the body of fog—then painting as a pure form does not exist; it is always but a more or less successful imitation of sculpture.

So instead of pictures, let there be painted sculpture, and let the roads stand somewhere at the edge of a wood, wound on huge wooden reels, like those used for electric cable.

I spend my time uselessly, so I shall not try to maintain that the occupation with such questions produces any benefits.[7]

Kataev seems to be speaking on more than one level here. He says that his thoughts are idle, but there is a strong suggestion that he considers them anything but useless. The meaning of life is one of the more serious themes that are interwoven throughout the work. Like Voznesensky, Kataev is intrigued by what lies beneath physical form, by that intangible "something else." Such "useless" questions as form and content, the meaning of time, the essence of literature, the reality of life, and the like, are subtly, often ambiguously presented throughout the text and form a philosophical subtext to these memoirs. When a writer is denied candid exposition on topics that interest him, he will eventually seek to circumvent this obstruction. Interspersed commentary, much like the separate units of a mosaic that form a pattern from afar, presents the far-sighted writer with a channel for communication. Such carefully constructed ambiguity becomes then a sort of cryptographical writing. The subtlety of some of Kataev's cryptography, camouflaged in surrealistic symbolism (painting as an imitation of sculpture) or in irony ("random observations of no special value"—that he nevertheless goes on to describe in significant detail) makes this work especially hard to interpret. We can at best only begin to unravel his images and his ideas.

From their idyllic retirement, the narrator and his wife go back in time. Missing their granddaughter, they suddenly find themselves back in the time when their daughter was eleven and their son nine. The narrator seems to question the "reality" of existence. "It's difficult to say what time of the year it was. And did it really happen? And if so, then in what dimension?" [8] This atmosphere of uncertainty is somewhat counter to the positive, directional mood prescribed by socialist realism. Here it prepares the way for an arbitrary mixing of summer and winter in the narrative, depending on the desired background and mood. The above excerpt continues:

> Such oversharp shadows, such overbright colors could mean either spring or the height of autumn, but judging by the thirst that tormented us all, it was probably summer, the very zenith of July. . . .

Thus the weather becomes an important part of the narrative, an almost impressionistic device to create the proper mood, to communicate a state of mind. The weather in the early bucolic scene is warm, sunny and mild, "spring was in the air." Later it is nearly always bleak and dismal, as if set in a winter of the author's discontent. As the family idyll fades, and with it the aura of peace and contentment, new dream-memories come forth. This time from way back in the past, from the narrator's youth, a recollection of a rainy evening in a Georgian restaurant with the poet Osip Mandelstam and his wife. The scene changes to a snowy night in Georgia, and the narrator remarks on the thin line between dream and memory:

> As a matter of fact, I didn't really dream this at all. It actually happened, but so painfully long ago, that it came to me now in the form of a distant, occasionally recurring dream that carried me back in a rosy haze of wine (and of course, under a lean moon) to that same legendary capital of carpets, the favorite province of the tetrarchs.[9] And what had once been not quite a dream, but rather a recollection, has now become a genuine dream, remarkable for its closeness to reality. For instance, the snow was quite real and huge flakes fell slowly and majestically, settling on the evergreen leaves of the magnolias. The whole city was coated with warm, southern snow.[10]

"A recollection [that] has now become a genuine dream" is a line that applies to several of the narrator's "dreams," especially his dream of America. The possible significances of this dream about Mandelstam, one of a number of talented writers who perished during the purges of the 1930's under the dreaded Georgian dictator, will not be discussed as it is not reflected in the image of America, our main concern here. One figure in the dream about Mandelstam, however, does reappear in the American narrative. This is the image of the "talking cat." Kataev continues Nekrasov's criticism of Soviet behavior in America, but is somewhat less candid than the latter. Kataev's comments are partially disguised in surrealistic technique and background, but are still clearly criticisms.

The first appearance of the "talking cat" is in a restaurant in Georgia where the narrator is attending a dinner party for writers and intellectuals. As talk subsides into drunken stupor, the host decides to enliven the party by treating his guests to a performance by his marvelous talking cat:

> The cat cringed and screwed up its eyes painfully. The host took its head in both hands, his thumbs together on top, his index fingers stuck expertly into the cat's mouth, stretching it. A tense and artificial smile appeared on the cat's childish face.
> "Speak!" the host commanded.
> The cat made a convulsive swallowing motion with its throat, opened its small, pink, triangular mouth, showing tiny teeth, and suddenly, in a forced mechanical voice said, quite distinctly, like a human, in the purest Russian:
> "Mama." [11]

By a similar manipulation the cat is also made to speak French *("Maman")*. The contrivance of the cat's utterances is matched by the enthusiastic applause of the guests:

"Unbelievable!" said the guests. "Unbelievable!
Astounding! What perfect pronunciation! What arti-
culation! What diction! Just like the Maly Academy
Theater! Or rather like the Art Theater!"

The image of the talking cat seems to be a caricature of
the puppet-like manipulations of Soviet writers and artists, and may be compared to Nekrasov's comment on
"dead water." The narrator later finds out that the cat
died during a rehearsal of the "simple Russian word
'neocolonialism'." [12]

Later, in the dream of America, Kataev continues
his attack against vulgar performances, especially in literature. In a cocktail party conversation with a Houston
woman, he defines his new literary school of *"mauvism."*
He tells her:

> . . . I am the founder of a completely new literary
> school of *mauvistes,* from the French word *mauvais*—
> bad. The essence of *mauvism* lies in the point that,
> since everybody writes very well nowadays, one must
> write badly, as badly as possible, so that people will
> pay some attention to you. Of course, it's not so easy
> to learn to write badly, because you'll have to sur-
> vive a devil of a lot of competition, but it's worth
> the effort. And if you learn to write really lousily,
> worse than everyone else, then your world fame is
> guaranteed. [13]

This passage offers another example of Kataev's
cryptographic doubletalk as he moves from the observation that "everyone writes very well nowadays" to the
remark that if you write badly, you'll have a lot of com-
petition, but the rewards are worthwhile. The woman,

a widow who discovered oil on her property and became a millionairess, is a caricature of *poshlost* and *nouveau riche* manners, but she also serves as a partial camouflage for Kataev's literary views. Kataev amplifies his philosophy of *mauvism* in a digression that appears earlier in the text:

> Maurois says that one cannot live simultaneously in two worlds—the real world and the world of the imagination, and that anyone who tries to do so suffers a fiasco. I am convinced that Maurois is mistaken. A fiasco is suffered by anyone who tries to live in only one of these two worlds. He is cheating himself, since he is denying himself exactly one-half of the beauty and wisdom of life.
>
> I have always lived in two dimensions. One without the other would be senseless to me. Their separation would immediately turn art either into abstraction or into a trivial process of recording life. Only a blending of these two elements can create an art that is truly beautiful. Perhaps this is the essence of *mauvism*.[14]

Kataev discusses *mauvism* in even greater length in his latest work, *The Herb of Oblivion*,[15] a more realistic memoir about his beginnings as a writer under the influence of Bunin. So there can be little doubt about his deep and serious interest in the concept, despite his overt pretenses to "idle" thoughts.

The "frightful dream" of the talking cat that interrupts the peace of the narrator's paradisaical afterlife is associated with another nightmare that always proceeds it: a "human woodpecker" by the name of Prokhindeykin, a sort of guardian-devil, follows the narrator like a shadow:

"We" means myself and another, let's say—person.
Truth to say, he's more a phantom, my strange companion who came with me to this territory, and who
now is as inseparable as my shadow, following a step
behind me. He's sort of an unnatural hybrid, a
human-woodpecker with a bony nose, clown-like eyes,
a corpulent swine—in the animal sense of the word—
a buffoon, a toady, an arch racketeer, an informer,
a bootlicker and an extortioner—a monstrous product of those far-off days.[16]

There is little impressionistic ambiguity in this passage. Kataev frequently indulges in such naturalistic caricature when criticizing Soviet failings. Prokhindeykin is
probably an exemplar of the spy-informer-opportunists
that were so prevalent in Soviet Russian during the thirties. He snoops everywhere, even around the old man at
the well. The narrator continues:

The old man was washing his bottles at the
Sacred Well, and he—my burdensome companion—
kept poking into everything, sniffing around, ready
to snatch any scrap and carry it off grimacing to his
stinking lair and bury it the way a dog buries a
chicken-foot, somewhere in a corner, under the Swed-
ish or Finnish sofa, or under a pouffe which itself
had been wheedled or swindled out of someone.

Prokhindeykin and the talking cat as will be noted, reappear to the narrator on Fifth Avenue in New York in
the person of one Alfred Parasyuk, a Soviet tourist.
    The "signals from the future" that Kataev keeps
referring to are another undercurrent motif in this work.

They begin, indirectly, in "paradise" when the narrator and his wife go riding in their automobile:

> Almost every day we got into a small car and sped along the highway past the strange painting and the road signs that resembled the works of abstract painters, although they had nothing in common with painting. None the less, they controlled our movements, warning us and letting us know in the symbolic language of their broken lines, zigzags, detours, triangles, and variously colored circles and stripes, about everything that lay ahead of us, that is in the not too distant future. Courbet once said: "That which we cannot see, the nonexistent and the abstract, does not belong to the realm of art." This is true, but it does belong to a realm of some kind. I believe, to a new realm, a fourth system of signals which is taking the place of the old. "Only writing and sound," says John Bernal, denying color this right, "embody human thought, and now computer systems and their codes can give completely new material shape to human thought, to some extent replacing language, and even going further than language in their development." [17]

The Sacred Well contains several references to this higher language that seems to be an outgrowth of intuition and sensory reception rather than logic. The "signals" are referred to many times in the work and occur as leitmotifs as well. They are primarily warning signals, indications of approaching harm—the zigzags and curves on the road of life:

> Signals from the future rushed toward us, warning us and warding off dangers that lay waiting at every turn of time.[18]

The first signals come when he feels the impending approach of old dreams and "futile remembrances.[11] He is afraid of dreaming again of the talking cat "or something even worse." But he does indeed dream of the cat, and Prokhindeykin. He also dreams of his friends, the Kozlovichi and the Ostrapenki, who are always en route somewhere, and of a trip of his own to America. The dream about America begins with a plane trip that is full of inauspicious presentiment for the narrator:

> I began to think about the continent I was slowly approaching and was seized by a presentiment of trouble, not too serious, but bad enough—something humiliating concerning my moccasins. Now I knew for certain that somewhere in New York there was a man who had been waiting for a long time to do me some harm. He wants to take something very precious away from me. My life? I don't know. Perhaps. I froze in advance, aware of my impotence and isolation, and I imagined myself coming face to face one fine day with this faceless man somewhere in the depths of an abstract New York street, deprived of all the objective details for which I have such a passion, both as a writer and as a man. My God, where are they taking me? [19]
>
> . . . . .
>
> All the while the presentiment of the colossal unpleasantness which I was approaching continued to grow and intensify in me. Obviously this was the result of irritations which the outside world inflicted on my nervous system. Let's call them signals from the future.[20]

The narrator notices three Americans on the airplane—three soldiers from an atomic unit stationed in

Holland. The portraits of two of the soldiers are briefly but pointedly drawn: one is in civilian clothes ("perhaps his uniform was burnt somewhere"), drinking from a flask of Vat 69 and flirting with the stewardess. The second soldier, sitting in the back of the plane, impresses the narrator only with his "dark, as if carbonized face" as he looks out the window. The third soldier is described at greater length:

> The Sergeant sat next to me. . . . He had a peaceful enough, well-intentioned look, but something about him worried me, some detail of his dress that I couldn't grasp, an ominous reminder, a signal of general danger. It was a faded little triangle of dark purple felt with some ominous red in it, with yellow lightning and the inscription "Spearhead," a patch sewn to the sleeve of his flying suit.
>
> Perhaps it was the mark of Cain for the nuclear age.[21]

This leitmotif, "the mark of Cain for the nuclear age," is carried throughout the work, and is perhaps the main "signal from the future"—the threat of atomic destruction. The description of the sergeant's arm patch recalls Kataev's descriptions of the road signs earlier in the work. This atomic warning signal is explicit in several direct references to atomic explosions, and implicit in the recurrent use of the adjectives "scorched" [*obuglennoe*] or "burnt" [*obgoreloe*] in highly unusual associations.

The first reference to this theme is found in a description of the narrator's nine-year-old playing war in the early part of the work:

The boy had reached the age when he no longer tormented cats, and instead ruined a great quantity of writing paper, first with drawings of air battles— burning airplanes with badly drawn swastikas on their wings, or tanks with rather well-shaped shells coming out of their guns; and then with identical repetitions of the same familiar face in profile with a black moustache and the elongated eyes of a hypnotist; and finally with monstrous, fantastic rolls, scribbles, lightning and ashes of an atomic explosion, labeled with a multicolored sign, *"kerosimo."* He was thrilled by everything. *Even by an atomic explosion.*[22]

The italicized sentence appears in the proofs, but was deleted in the published version. The misspelling *"kerosimo"* leads to another memory, that of a squabble his son and daughter had over the contents of a yellow *kvas* wagon. After drinking their refreshing fill of *kvas* on that hot summer day (though the daughter stubbornly persists in calling it kerosine), the narrator comments on the heat:

We had barely been able to endure the airlessness, the dreadful, indescribable heat which seemed as if it might have come from Hiroshima. It even felt as though our clothes were beginning to carbonize.[23]

The reference to "carbonized clothing" is a somewhat unusual association with summer heat, where one's clothes are more likely to be wet from perspiration than burntdry.

On page 39 he speaks of the "turbid shadows of atomic submarines carrying nuclear rockets" in the Atlantic Ocean off the coast of America. On page 63 he mentions "sensing" the presence of underground atomic tests in Nevada. And on page 31, he describes Picasso's "Guernica"—a mural depicting a scene from the Spanish Civil War—as a portrayal of "universal atomic destruction."

The modifiers "scorched" and "burnt," describing parts of the body, articles of clothing, and objects such as books, money, and cars, occur some twenty times.[24] The ending of the work is an atomic disintegration and fallout simulation as the narrator returns from the plane of his dreams to the reality of his hospital bed.

Kataev's impressions of America are somewhat ambiguous, perhaps intentionally so after the sharp criticisms that rewarded Nekrasov's candor. His impressions of nocturnal New York from the air and on the ground are painted in terms that recall Gorky's "City of the Yellow Devil" with its repetitive and vivid hyperbole:

> At a fantastic distance below me floated nocturnal New York which in spite of all its brilliance was not able to turn night into day, so powerfully black was this night. And in the darkness of this unknown continent, in its mysterious depths, someone was patiently waiting for me, poised and ready to do me harm. Me, a lonely traveler, suddenly thrown over here from another world, not the old world, but perhaps one even newer than this one.
>
> Oh, if you only knew how lonely and defenseless I felt, coming down the two-storey high steps, as I entered the purplish-green inferno of the near-tropical New York night—oppressive, humid, airless. I walked along the uniformly lit corridors of the customs building, corridors that seemed cut into the frozen body of an iceberg, where, lit from all sides,

I had no shadow. But the air was "conditioned" so
that for a few minutes I could enjoy the artificial
cool. Then under the gaze of a beautiful customs
girl, a smart blonde with the self-assured eyes of a
film star and with a pistol in her white holster, I
took my slow-moving suitcase from the illuminated
conveyor belt and once again plunged into the nocturnal purplish-green heat. No kind of artificial light
could possibly dispel for me the blackness of the
infernal, almost tropic August midnight of an unknown continent, where instead of Centigrade, the
temperature was shown as Fahrenheit, which ex-
aggerated it monstrously so that the damp heat
seemed even more unbearable.[25]

The feeling of a vast darkness waiting to swallow
the lonely traveler from another "newer" world, and
the purplish-green infernal heat that seems even hotter
because it is measured on the Fahrenheit scale seem to
set the mood for the dream of America.[26] However, this
bathetic confrontation of the lonely, minuscule traveler
with the overwhelming environs of America may also
be a grotesque satire on the Gorkianesque style of propaganda. What seems to be a derogatory comment on
the iceberg-like cold of the air conditioning does not
detract from the existence of that air conditioning, especially to a technology-conscious Soviet reading public.
Also, the lack of extensive customs searching and the description of the customs guard as a beautiful blonde
could be interpreted as a backhanded compliment. Kataev
describes the air conditioning of his hotel room as a
"sepulchral wind," claiming that the room is not really
air-conditioned because there is only a "box" in the
window that one must turn on for oneself. This slightly
antagonistic tone may be but another example of "double-

talk"—the technological accomplishments are self-evident. A more detailed example of this ambiguous portrayal occurs later when Kataev describes his fully automated hotel room in Houston:

> At the head of my mechanical bed there was a remote-control panel so that, without getting up, I could program the life process of my hotel room. By simply pressing a button I could regulate the temperature and the humidity of the room. I could learn the weather forecast, the atmospheric pressure, the latest stock market quotations, the sports schedules, the trotting races program, the latest news, and finally, I could have myself awakened at any specified time, although time as such does not really exist. I was simultaneously man and dwelling, there was so much in common between us, beginning with the regulated temperature of our bodies, and ending with the prearranged hour of waking. The room awoke first, and then the occupant—if he wasn't already awake from insomnia.[27]

The narrator almost merges with the living organism of his hotel room. The luxuriousness of the room is quite vividly conveyed, although again, Kataev does not exclaim how wonderful it is. He relies instead on subtle, ambiguous descriptions and seems to be wary of stating his intentions and impressions as explicitly as did Nekrasov. In other passages he completely incorporates himself into various objects he sees. At one point he says so directly: "Here I made the discovery that man possesses the magical ability to turn instantly into the object he is observing."[28] This may be a literary device to facilitate the descriptions of several things: his hotel, a highway, an automobile, a department store, and even the Texas soil. It might be noted here that one usually does not project himself into things that he dislikes. So that while Kataev does not really say whether he likes these things or not, the feeling is that he is impressed by what he sees. There is a comfortable interrelationship with the object that creates a favorable atmosphere and leaves an impression more positive than negative. Voznesensky's surrealistic poem "New York Bird" and his "self-portrait" ("New York Night Airport") may play a role in Kataev's style and mood in these passages.

Kataev also describes a "superfunctional" department store in Houston:

> But what is the point, you ask yourself, of building this department store, a marvel of engineering and architectural skill, the acme of simplicity and comfort, free from any modernistic decorations or gimmicks, inordinately large and flat, with well-lit ceilings, lawns and flower beds set in the black and white marble of its vast floors, a store that conveniently and attractively stores and displays in its compartments millions of items ranging from the essential to those of minimal usefulness? [29]

What is the point, one may ask, of such a detailed exposition of good features, except perhaps an indirect compliment? The last reference to the abundance of merchandise on the shelves of the store cannot fail to impress the Soviet reader who spends much of his time waiting in queues in front of the nearly empty shelves of Soviet stores.

On a walk through a suburb of Washington Kataev comments that the private homes, stores, service stations, lighted streets and so forth remind him of an exhibition. Perhaps this is an oblique reference to some of the United States Information Agency exhibitions that have visited the Soviet Union with displays of American life. Again the author is noncommittal, but once again, the things he mentions speak for themselves.

The narrator's first day in New York is full of inauspicious signals. He almost fatalistically heads toward oncoming disaster:

> I was no longer conscious of where I was going and what I was doing. I was led, as they used to say in the old days, by the mysterious force of destiny. But in reality, I was obeying the signals coming from my environment. I went from street to street, crossing narrow squares, straight into the trap set for me in one of the thoroughfares of that fairly old city of brick construction. At every step I was confronted by scenes and pictures that I interpreted as signals of distress. The sloven emptiness of these poor districts frightened me. I had no doubt but that somewhere near, maybe even around this brick corner, I would be robbed. But what could they get from me that was of any value? A yellow vaccination certificate and forty paper dollars with slightly scorched corners, securely pinned into my inside pocket. I wouldn't give them up even if someone stuck a silent automatic pistol in my guts from that nearby telephone booth.[30]

The narrator's presentiment is rewarded by an encounter with an Italian shoeshine man who materializes mysteriously out of the distance, together with his shoeshine shack, and blatantly defrauds the narrator of 50¢

for a 25¢ shine "which could be done by a Negro in the subway for 10¢." Kataev devotes an inordinate amount of space to this episode, almost five full pages. The contrast between the slightly paranoiac tone of the narrator here and the triviality of the incident may be intended by the author as a satirical exaggeration on the theme of exploitation and robbery in America. The sense of the ridiculous that Kataev imparts to some of his descriptions about America may also be satirical answers to some of the questions that Nekrasov was criticized for refusing to consider: "Is it true that in New York a crime is committed every six minutes? that the temperature goes up to 100° in the shade? that one in every four Americans owns a car?" The first question may be reflected in the scene with the Italian shoeshine man; the second, in the description of the New York heat on an August night; and the third, in a passage that describes the occupants of two large limousines—one with a lady in a polka-dotted dress with her polka-dotted dog, and the other containing only a chauffeur and a newly pressed suit.[31] The robbery scene ends with a mawkish plaint:

> I felt so sorry for myself that I was ready to lie down on the hot sidewalk next to a rather weathered brick wall under an iron fire escape and cry out to all of Tenth Avenue that I'd been cheated, robbed, tricked, like the world's biggest sucker. But what could I do? Nothing! I couldn't even complain to the U.N. General Assembly, whose smooth glass edifice rose up like a Swedish bookcase above the iron bridges and concrete supports of East River Drive: for I didn't have the status of even the most underdeveloped country.
> I was only a private individual.[32]

The notion of complaining to the United Nations over a fifty-cent shoeshine can only be a tongue-in-cheek satire of the propagandists' tales. It also allows him to slip in a nice description of the United Nations Building, which is not visible from Tenth Avenue. Kataev's comment that the free enterprise system allows fluctuating tariffs for shoeshines would seem to support this satirical approach. If he were seriously interested in exposing economic exploitation in America, he would not have selected so trivial an example.

With the "great robbery" out of the way, the narrator then reports spending a magnificent day in New York. An acquaintance picks him up in a rented blue Cadillac convertible, and they drive around Manhattan. Kataev describes the ride in a delightful impressionistic passage:

> . ., . we flew out into the sunlight, careened around dizzy bends, headed back and drove with the speed of sound across the new George Washington suspension bridge compared with which the famous Brooklyn Bridge once admired by Mayakovsky is nothing; we flew through the middle of the suspended structure like a fly through a huge harp with white strings.[33]

Kataev, like Voznesensky, finds a new structure to admire as Mayakovsky once esteemed the Brooklyn Bridge.

In the middle of an impressionistic description of New York's Fifth Avenue in midwinter, the narrator suddenly spies an old friend:

> . . . this setting was completely natural for the somewhat fantastic appearance of a man who suddenly

arose beside me on the steps of the library like a fourth lion with portentously raised eyebrows. I think he was one of a series of reincarnations of the late talking cat, or even, still worse, of my former burdensome companion—if you remember him—the human woodpecker, who had grown somewhat bald. At that moment I felt his hot breath and heard his voice, distorted by time and space, secretly mutter in my ear: "I must warn you to be more careful. No need to admire everything so openly. What's so great about that George Washington Bridge of theirs? It's crap! It's just like our Crimea Bridge, only a little longer. Better be extremely careful about your opinions, or you'll be involved in a provocation before you know it." [34]

Kataev appears to be continuing Nekrasov's criticisms of Soviet manners abroad. The author's use of vulgar slang terms such as "muttered" [zabubnivšij] and "crap" [der'ma] is significant in that it emphasizes the low manners and speech of the character portrayed. The absence of such vulgarisms in other parts of the work seems to indicate some such intent on the part of the author.

As we have noted with Nekrasov, this use of the American scene to voice a personal complaint about Soviet visitors abroad is one of the most striking changes in the writing style of the sixties, and is part of the complex cryptography that drifts in and out of works on foreign travels, especially in America. Here, the narrator deplores the crudity of some "professional" Soviet tourists who are sent abroad to spy and to inform. One is reminded of Nekrasov's plea for naturalness and spontaneity when meeting people, as well as his complaints about the group leader and guardian, Ivan Ivanovich. Kataev's "tourist" relates one of his misadventures in America:

If you want to know, I myself suffered a lot, I really got burned. Just imagine the scene—they send me to America, to the City of the Yellow Devil. . . . I arrive, order some visiting cards in the dimestore, dress like a man of the world, hire a car on credit, and so forth. . . . Everything's O.K.! I get an invitation to dinner. I go. Here's the set-up: a business lunch in the Palm Court of the Waldorf Astoria. . . . My nerves, of course, are strained, but I don't let on, and act the perfect gentleman. And what do you think! The bastards trapped me with a provocation. Lunch is over and waiters in white silk stockings serve crystal finger bowls. Now, you understand, I wasn't born yesterday. I'm not fooled easily. I know what's going on. I'm a scholar. I've read the instructions: if they give you a bowl of water after lunch, for heaven sakes don't drink it, because it's not lemonade but for rinsing your fingers. Some of our fellows have really been burned by that experience, but not me. So I take the bowl, and start to wash my hands for all to see. But it turned out to be a pineapple compote. Just think of it! In full view of the whole Waldorf Astoria I washed my hands in a pineapple compote. It even turned slightly blue, almost purple.

Well, of course they sent for me and said: "Fedya, you didn't do too well in the City of the Yellow Devil. We'll have to send you to some other continent. . . ."

He rummaged in his briefcase and pulled out a small visiting card with embossed lettering on which was printed in Latin letters: "Alfred Parasyuk, intellectual."

Talking cat! Talking cat! [35]

The caricature here is a masterful exercise in humorous satire, and recalls the ornamental prose of some of

Kataev's early writings, as well as the satirical style of Ilf and Petrov. The passage leaves little doubt as to the author's feelings about contrived behavior, and calls to mind Nekrasov's advice to "just be yourself."

Kataev's criticism of the Soviet Union in this work provides a sharp commentary on the immoral and uncivilized behavior of some of his countrymen. A naturalistic portrait reminiscent of former Party Chairman Khrushchev is included in a description of various television programs the narrator watches in his hotel room:

> Then there was the performance of a world-famous Russian eccentric with the pot-bellied figure of a *vanka-vstanka*[36] and a stupidly hypocritical smile on his ill-tempered, gap-toothed mouth. He was showing off his best trick—the art of placing his hard crowned felt hat on his bald head as though it were an inverted chamber pot, supported only by his ears. He had done this four times and was just about to take his bow, when suddenly a leg came out, kicked him in the backside, and sent him flying from the scene.[37]

But there can be no doubt as to Kataev's deep attachment to his homeland, which is tenderly referred to in several lyrical strains. In one place he mentions the deep homesickness that comes over him abroad: "I had sometimes had a similar feeling before, not often, but almost every time I found myself beyond the borders of my homeland. I am very prone to a rather desperate and incomparable homesickness."[38] In another passage his Gogolian lyricism comes strongly to the fore:

> Amidst the fields, meadows and woods there was a hint of chemical factories, rocket-launching sites and

the catapults of high-voltage power lines traversing in every direction the unique, inimitable, thrice-blessed country of my soul which has given me so many delights, so many upward flights, falls, disappointments, so many joys, sublime thoughts, great and small achievements, so much love and hatred, occasional despair, poetry, music, crude intoxication and divinely subtle technicolor dreams that came to me so sweetly and tenderly at dawn to the timid singing of the first nightingales—in a word, so much of everything that has made me what I am . . .[39]

Two pages later he again refers to the "country of my soul," and four pages after that to the "garden of my soul." This strong emotional tie to the motherland is a typical feature of Russian writing from Gogol to the present day.

As the narrator flies back from America, the return to his homeland is paralleled by a return to life on the operating table:

Now, as I was returning home from the land of Stravinsky to the land where they have turned Schubert inside out, gradually, second by second, the time that had vanished without explanation when I flew there across the ocean, returned. Breath by breath, the life that had been sunk in hypnotic sleep also returned.

Well, I know now this dim lake of Auber,
This misty mid-region of Nod [meaning Weir].

—And the movement of monsters in the sea, and the growth of the vine in the valley—[40]

The reference to the "land of Stravinsky" refers to America—while in California he notes a strong wind blowing from Mexico:

> . . . over the villa of Stravinsky whose name itself is just like a wintry blast from the depths of Mexico with all the wind, string, percussion and pizzicato instruments joined together in a counterpoint of genius . . .[41]

The concession to Stravinsky's genius is significant in a country that officially disapproves of "modern" music. The land of inverted Schubert is the Soviet Union—at a cocktail party in Houston a woman asks him about the famous Soviet composer who brilliantly turned Schubert's "Ave Maria" inside out to create an original song for a popular Soviet movie. This may be a reference to Prokoviev's score for "Lieutenant Kije." It is not clear whether the irony here is intentional. The couplet is from Edgar Alan Poe's ballad, "Ulalume," and will be discussed below. The last two lines are a couplet from Pushkin's poem "The Prophet," several lines of which are scattered surrealistically throughout the text,[42] implying a concrete philosophical association with the poem. This, too, will be discussed later.

Kataev set out in search of the "real America," but he did not succeed in finding it. Americans themselves do not seem to know where the real America lies:

> Then I realized that there isn't a single American who is sure that he lives in the real America. He is convinced that somewhere in another state there exists some sort of a real, genuine America, his promised land. It is hard for him to believe that the place

in which he lives is, in fact, that great and world-famous America.[43]

This passage offers another example of Kataev's ambiguity. It is difficult to tell whether he is criticizing America, or noting the rich variety of the country and the impossibility of typifying or stereotyping it. A few lines later he compounds the confusion by claiming he had not really come in search of America, but to see a woman he had loved long ago:

> Nowhere had I been able to find the real and genuine America—which, by the way, I had not actually been looking for. Now I can admit this. For me America was the last hope of possibly seeing once more a woman whom I had loved since childhood.[44]

This may be another cryptographical device to outwit the censor. It is hard to believe one would travel so far and see so much merely to prepare for a meeting with an old flame. After his visit is over he says: "Now America almost completely ceased to interest me. She seemed to have lost her soul, and reminded me of a beautiful artificial country like Disneyland. Why had I been so eager to come here?"

The woman, who remains unnamed, and her story that is related throughout the American dream, may well be an allegory—perhaps of the narrator's search for his soul. In some ways the woman is an image of time—the flow of time and the accompanying disillusionment in the ideals of youth. The memories of his young love are tenderly recaptured in the text, interwoven with the descriptions of his travels as he moves from city to city. He describes his visit to her home:

> From afar I saw her motionless figure, although in the dusk she merged almost completely with the bare, iron-black bush growing in front of her small, single-storied home. It seemed as though she had been waiting for me here forever, from time immemorial, and had already turned into a small grey statue. This thought did not strike me as strange because the formal measurement of time, artificially divorced from space, and its commonly accepted division into years, days, hours, minutes and centuries, provides only a conditional and distorted idea of true time.[46]

After an evening of catching up on the forty years they had not seen each other, the ideal of the past seems to fade in confrontation with the reality of the present, as the narrator realizes that you can't go home again:

> . . . and this whole unnecessary, contrived meeting seemed to me like a painful immersion into the depths of an infinitely deep sea dividing us with the heavy water of silence through which our words were exchanged with difficulty, sometimes reaching consciousness like some sort of acoustical hallucination, and sometimes dissolving without a trace somewhere on the verge of consciousness like undreamed dreams that leave no traces in the memory.[47]

The intricate expression and imagery in this passage suggest a deeper meaning, a cryptographical reference to the ideals of the narrator's youth. A poignant parting scene with the woman seems to allude to this possibility as well. After a tenderly written episode in which the woman relates the story of her father's love for the narrator's mother, she tells him:

> "I would not have recognized you on the street, but I would have on a train. When they told me that you had been shot, I went home, sat on the divan and turned to stone. I couldn't even cry. I was completely numb. I couldn't bend my fingers. I felt as though I'd turned into a piece of marble. Nothing existed around me any longer. What a joy to find out that it wasn't true, that you're alive, you're alive."
>
> "But perhaps it is true after all, and I've been dead for a long time."
>
> "That would mean we've both been dead."
>
> "Perhaps we have."
>
> And he tore out my sinful tongue.[48]

The last sentence is another line from Pushkin's poem. Once again we see the difficulty of deciphering the author's meaning. He could be alluding to a spiritual death. The inclusion of the Pushkin line here in the text strengthens the argument for a cryptographical theme of spiritual catharsis and transfiguration. Kataev's radically new approach to literature reinforces this supposition as well.

Whatever else the woman might signify, she becomes an excuse, a device to help escape the inevitable political reporting expected of Soviet writers in America so that the author could concentrate on a personal journey (which is probably also the reason he selected the form of fictionalized narrative instead of the usual travel-memoir format). The woman may be a metaphor for the author's soul. She might also be interpreted as a stand-in for America—the two images are directly associated in the passage below. Or she may be nothing more than a lyrical recollection of a real event in the author's life, though the embellishments of her image, already noted, do suggest something more. The Russian woman's husband had died the year before, and as the end of the visit nears she says: "I have no one left here. No one at all. I can live well enough, but I am completely alone." Her words strike the narrator as he continues:

That was the last thing I heard her say, and those pitiful words pursued me day and night, first in the canyons of Nevada where perhaps at that very moment they were carrying out underground nuclear tests that were inaudible on the outside, but which I could sense through the stronger beating of my heart that shocked my entire neurovascular system. Then they followed me through the iron girders of Chicago, in the morning winter twilight of its gangster slums, in the coal-black recesses between the old skyscrapers and the newest sixty-story lamellate spiral towers of two buildings of inexpensive apartments. They stood alongside the incredibly long shoreline and were shrouded in the clouds of frozen mist which constantly crept over the city from Lake Michigan, whose presence one could only vaguely discern by the ice on one's eyelashes, by its metallic mother-of-pearl glimmer, and by the strong northern wind which stung one's face with the burning cold of the unseen lake, turned to stone by the Canadian frost and the icy wastes of the Arctic. And finally, those pitiful words pursued me through the respectable brick homes and churches which give Boston a special, almost religious austerity and its air of tedium . . .[49]

This association of the woman's words with America is interesting. Is America a widow as well? Kataev describes the poet Robert Frost at the 1961 Inauguration ceremonies as a representative of the old America offering his congratulations to the representative of the new America, President Kennedy. The assassination of Kennedy is an important motif in the work. However, the above passage seems to be emphasizing the loneliness and fear of man in general, man who spends his time making atomic bombs for destruction. Both Voznesensky and Nekrasov have commented on this matter before. Note that the narrator *feels* the underground explosions in Nevada (and probably elsewhere as well). The words "I am alone" follow him through the unpleasant parts of Chicago where the wintry winds blow down from the Artic. (If they blow south over America, they are probably blowing southward over the other side of the world as well.) The ambiguity of this impressionistic passage again suggests a deeper meaning, a metaphysical plane that becomes more apparent on the next page as the narrator describes his visit with the dying poet Robert Frost in Boston. The poet speaks:

> "Mankind, listen to what I have to say. In the name of higher truth, if universal madness should begin, don't poison the wells, leave the apples on the trees so that the people may satisfy their thirst and hunger if you don't want life to disappear forever from the earth." [50]

The warning not to poison the wells so that life may continue adds a symbolic nuance to the title of the work, the "sacred" well of humanity, which were it to be poi-

soned would contaminate the bottles as well, the endless
bottles—human beings? On another level, the sacred
well could be a metaphor for the author's soul; the bottles, his thoughts. Curiously enough, the words he attri-
butes to Frost seem untypical of that poet's more stoic
temperament. For example, in "The Lesson for Today,"
written during another gloomy time in history, 1940,
Frost says:

> If this uncertain age in which we dwell
> Were really as dark as I hear sages tell,
> And I convinced that they were really sages,
> I should not curse myself with it to hell,
> But leaving not the chair I long have sat in
> I should betake me back ten thousand pages
> To the world's undebatably dark ages,
>
> . . . . .
>
> Earth's a hard place in which to save the soul,
> And could it be brought under state control,
> So automatically we all were saved,
> Its separateness from Heaven could be waived;

The presence of death accompanies the narrator
through America but is especially evident in Washington,
D.C. (Kataev visited the city the year before the assassination of Kennedy in Dallas.) The weather is unpleasant
—"melancholy grey winter days"—as the narrator sees
apparitions in Arlington: an Indian with a tomahawk,
George Washington and other spirits wandering among
the graves "while President Kennedy sleeps peacefully
in the White House." A few lines later, after the comment on his deep homesickness, he mentions that the
feeling of death seems to be with him all the time now.

While walking in a suburb of Washington he notices an especially inviting-looking home:

> Most of all I liked a small private house set back in an unfenced garden with a faultless lawn and two evergreen magnolias with layers of light snow on their dark, glossy leaves. The house was a delightful yellowish pink, like Turkish delight, with a Christmas wreath of mistletoe over the front door, and two torch-shaped glass lamps glowing wanly in the evening dusk. The windows of the house were covered with white blinds lit from inside by a welcoming festive light. I immediately thought how nice and cosy it must be in this house where joyful hosts were awaiting their guests; or perhaps the guests had already come and were now sitting at an old Chippendale mahogany table before a Limoges dish of plum pudding glowing with the blue flame of Jamaican rum.[51]

This cozy-looking home turns out to be a funeral parlor! The irony here may be intended to emphasize the contrast between appearance and reality, a theme that greatly interests Kataev in this work. Inside, he sees many America coffins like those he had seen before in films and the theater, and once on television as a flag-draped coffin stopped at the door of a cathedral where a Catholic bishop in his "ominously divided mitre" awaited it. This is another reference to the assassination which the narrator says he foresaw on the television set in his hotel room in Houston. This *déjà-vu*/prescience theme runs through the American dream. Another example is found on page 38: "Through some completely mysterious visual associations, I unmistakably recognized cities I had never seen before." It appears to be a device to afford grounds for various comments by the author.

The narrator then describes the shooting of Kennedy and of Oswald, and the sight of Jacqueline Kennedy riding in the ambulance with her husband's body. She is described in especially touching terms:

> Her face, shown in close-up, was beautiful and motionless, with wide-set, dark eyes and a short, slightly turned-up nose. Her head filled the screen for a while and then quickly, like a schoolgirl, Jacqueline gathered the folds of her coat and jumped into the seat beside the chauffeur. She was wearing a very short skirt, according to the fashion of the season, and it revealed the well-formed legs of the young, wealthy, happy American woman who still did not quite realize that she was now a widow . . .[52]

This is a very compassionate portrait of a millionairess, the wife of the political leader of a capitalist country. The death of President Kennedy, presented by the narrator as a "premonition," seems to be an ominous "signal" for America. This fatalistic attitude toward America is also felt in Kataev's comments on the Negro problem:

> I understood that as long as black and white live side by side in America without merging or recognizing each other, and enjoying only formal equality as citizens of this immeasurably rich and cruel country, where tradition rules over law, where a white policeman may shoot a black boy with impunity, and a whole people have been deprived of their rights as free men—the United States will be the most unhappy country in the world, like a wealthy

man stricken with cancer: there is no salvation or cure for him.[53]

This passage offers a good example of the direct and unambiguous commentary that occasionally drifts into the dream narrative. The author also makes some statements here that border on propaganda (a white policeman may shoot Negroes with impunity).

The only other Negro mentioned in *The Sacred Well* is an elegantly dressed one "with the refined intelligent features of a European" whom the narrator imagines to be a doctor:

> Perhaps my Negro companion was a doctor who had rejected the psychoanalytical approach of the "great Freud" to functional psychic disorders and was conducting research into purely medicinal methods for the cure and prevention of neurological and psychic disorders on behalf of some powerful pharmaceutical corporation.[54]

It is interesting that Kataev describes him as a researcher into chemical means for treating psychic disorders instead of following the functional approach of Freud. The inference here is not clear. This Negro is sitting in the first class compartment of a plane to Washington. The narrator and a white general are the only other passengers. The general is described as "an ordinary American general" who reminds the narrator of "Wrangel or Kolchak, or one of the other counterrevolutionary generals of the Intervention Period"—the Vietnamese war literally reflected in his eyes.

The Negro and the general are united by fate as the hapless victims of "an ancient national crime":

These two citizens of the United States, so different from one another in appearance, were bound to each other by the unbreakable bonds of an ancient crime for which neither of them was to blame. They were united by all the might of the American government even more securely than the phases of earth time, which on our planet exist simultaneously, chasing on each other's heels: white day and black night with all her senseless dreams and suppressed desires.[55]

The comparison of the relations of the two races to the eternal chase of day and night is an arresting analogy but what the author means by the "senseless dreams" of black night is not clear. He does not seem optimistic about the race problem in America. In yet another passage he speaks of this "crime":

This is a retribution for the crime of their ancestors who reduced a whole people to slavery, deprived them of a homeland and left a terrible legacy to their descendants. The freed slaves are still slaves because America has not become their home.[56]

The narrator reminds us that he is from another world, one completely different from the world of the Negro and the general. But he could be referring as much to a world of the spirit as to the material world.

In another passage, after viewing the film "West Side Story," the narrator, moved by the sight of the young Americans in the audience crying over the tragic fate of the young lovers in the film, says that from that moment he loved America, but only a certain part of her:

At that moment I fell in love with America.
Not the country of latter-day caesars in demo-

cratic jackets and broad-brimmed Stetson hats, a country that seems to be but a modern version of the great Roman Empire with all its crude statues and monuments, its stadiums, hippodromes, mausoleums, and *curule aediles,* the marble seats of its lawgivers, the grandiose obelisks reflected in the long mirrors of rectangular lakes among the hills of the Indian forest reserve and the English lawns of Washington. The city lifts the high misty papal tiara of its anti-artistic Capitol dome into the pale North American winter sky as though it were affirming to the whole Western hemisphere the bitter truth once uttered by my friend Henri Barbusse that all domes, even the most magnificent, are simply ridiculous, like candle snuffers.[57]

Kataev's description of America as a new Roman Empire is rather severe. However, the country of monuments, stadiums, and mausoleums might be a cryptographical reference to the Soviet Union. Yevtushenko has subtly equated the Soviet Union with the Roman Empire in a recent poem, "By the Forgotten Roman Way," discussed in the next chapter. The narrator continues:

I fell in love with the America of the Washington students, those boys and girls who wept in the technicolor darkness of the matinee over the broken and desecrated love of the white Romeo and the dark-skinned Juliet, and perhaps over their own defenseless youth as well.

I understood the tragedy of a great country that has chosen the path of Rome, not the path of Athens.

The American dream ends as the narrator is met by his wife at the airport and they set off "as though nothing had happened" along a forgotten street where, from an old man in "burnt" [*obgorelye*] gloves, they buy some "roasted" [*obuglennye*] chestnuts and eat them, easily peeling the "scorched" [*obuglennye*] shells. The use of these "burnt/scorched" descriptions is significant here, even though in this particular context they are fully natural, because their consistent use throughout the work in unconventional associations has given them power to evoke the underlying theme of atomic destruction.

The ending of the story, the scene of transition from "dream" to "reality," is masterfully written. It is both a simulation of an atomic disintegration of matter that culminates the atomic leitmotifs of the story, and a symbolic purification of the author's soul. The narrator loses consciousness as all matter around him disintegrates into dust particles:

> And from the colorless, no longer existent sky fell a strange, invisible, intangible substance, the product of some sort of disintegration.[58]

He then ends his voyage through the realm of dream and reminiscence, and returns to consciousness on the operating table:

> "Let's go back," my wife managed to say, having become completely transparent, diffuse and motionless, like a dream or rather like the memory of a dream. She pressed up against my shoulder, melting and losing substance before my eyes, and I realized that we would not be going anywhere, because I could not remember the name of that evergreen

plant which was covered in midwinter with very bright crimson flowers, and only that could save us. Beyond the grey shroud of the sky, flying into the vastness of the world, silently raging and licking the Universe on all sides, a strange flame of decaying matter, invisible, intangible, cold and at the same time spreading the sharp unpleasant fresh smell of rust, the smell of oxygen which, it turns out, I had been breathing for some time through rubber tubes inserted deep into my nostrils. I could hear the oxygen bubbles whispering through the gauze over my lips, and I realized fairly clearly that I was no longer asleep but that I was lying on a high surgical bed in my ward, and that the black blood dripping into the bottle was my own blood, that outside the window the garden of my soul was in flower, that the narrow-eyed anaesthetist had not forgotten to wake me up, that man cannot die until he has been born, nor be born without having died; and that not far away, beside the Sacred Well, most likely just as before, the familiar old man was standing and patiently washing his bottles.[59]

The old man may be a symbol of the continuity of life no matter what experiences, real or imagined, confront the human soul. His supply of bottles is endless, "like eternity":

> My wife, shrugging her shoulders, said that it wasn't really a sack, but a common, ordinary bottomless pit, like the bottomless pit of time, in other words —eternity.[60]

Kataev's arresting description of the sack as a "common, ordinary" bottomless pit is typical of his surrealistic

style in this work, and reinforces the cryptographical possibilities of the image. The old man is mentioned once
more in the beginning of the story washing his bottles
without interruption despite the fact that Prokhindeykin
is snooping. *The Sacred Well* thus ends on a note of
resignation and peace—the author's fears seem at last
laid to rest (the tumor removed; the patient restored to
life, "reborn").

This final passage seems to be a recapitulation of
the narrator's voyage through dream and memory. The
image of the poinsettia (the "evergreen" covered with
bright crimon flowers in winter) is an elusive one. It is
mentioned several times in the work. The narrator notices
the flower growing in California in winter and it seems
to become a symbol of something beyond his reach. He
can never remember its name, even though he feels it is
vital to man's survival. Later he refers to it as "the word
that will save us all." The poinsettia is a Christmas flower
in the Western Hemisphere, and as such it might possibly
be a symbol for Christianity—a concern with the spiritual
life of man in this materialistic age. Kataev also seems
preoccupied with disintegrating matter, the matter that
time dissolves and remolds:

> . . . one gets a much better idea of time not from
> the sand trickling imperceptibly from one half of an
> hour glass to the other, but from a simple stone
> changing "in the flow of time" into sand, or gradu-
> ally changing back from sand into stone, and then
> again "in the flow of time" becoming sand, because
> one can not only feel but actually see the destructive
> or creative action of time unseparated from matter.[61]

Before regaining consciousness the narrator reports

the sight of a "strange flame of decaying matter" destroying the universe. Perhaps this is materialism. Kataev's surrealism effectively obscures the significance of his images here as he subtly switches to another plane: the *invisible* flame becomes a rusty *smell,* then the smell and *sound* of oxygen as the narrator awakens to the *visible* world in his hospital bed. The end of the passage (one long sentence in Russian) recapitulates an important cryptographical theme: metaphysical rebirth ("man can not die without having been born, nor be born without having died"). The last half of this aphorism is a puzzling one for a materialistic philosophy like Communism, and seems to stress Kataev's divergence from certain tenets of that philosophy.

The operation itself, besides serving as the frame of the narration and pretext for the unorthodox flights of fancy, might also be interpreted as a symbol of the author's psychical exploration of his soul, a procedure paralleling the physical operation on his body. The continual interpolations into his "dreams" of the operating process, in a way that contrasts, instead of complementing or fitting in with the dream text, suggest this possibility. For example, the following paragraph occurs in the midst of a dream about his friends the Kozlovichi:

> Perhaps my uncovered body was lying somewhere in another dimension and under the operating lights blue figures were examining my ancient scars: bullet wounds, shrapnel scars, and the marks of various illnesses, wars and revolutions.[62]

Perhaps the author is examining the scars and wounds of his soul. In another passage about the human woodpecker, Prokhindeykin, he writes:

We were like two convicts chained to the same ball. I was dying, stumbling, but he—my burdensome companion—mericlessly pushed me further and further on. He became a disease, he nestled himself somewhere inside me, in a secret cavity of my guts, or perhaps even lower; he was a painfully swelling tumor, an adenoma of the prostrate, continually poisoning my blood which throbbed convulsively and sullenly in my aorta, barely able to make the muscle of my worn-out heart contract.

If only the tumor could be removed quickly! [63]

This may be an allusion to a spiritual catharsis, an attempt to free his spirit and his art from the "tumor" of the censor, or even the "tumor" of his lesser self. Prokhindeykin may thus be a symbol of the evil extant in the author's environs, or a double of the sinful side of his own soul. The identification of Prokhindeykin with the poisonous tumor suggests a personal contact.

In another passage Kataev surrealistically touches on the theme of the Crucifixion:

—If I were, for instance, a liquid—say a small sluggish river—then I wouldn't have to be lifted from the stretcher onto the operating table. A slight tilting of space and I could simply be poured from one plane to another, and then my tormented body all the same would reproduce the classical, diagonally broken posture of the deposition from the cross: head hanging down, legs collapsed, and the hollow-ribbed body hanging at an angle in the arms of disciples— [64]

There is little that can be deciphered conclusively in this passage, except that it has strong religious overtones. The author may again be referring to the theme of death and (spiritual) resurrection. The narrator's tenderest memory of prerevolutionary Russia takes place on Easter Day, when the young girl he loved kissed him in greeting, exchanging the customary Russian Orthodox salutation: "Christ is risen!" [65] The narrator is remembering the kiss; the author may be remembering Easter.

Kataev's selection of lines from Pushkin's poem, "The Prophet" is also significant. The poem begins: "Tormented by a spiritual thirst / I wandered in a gloomy desert." Although these lines are not quoted by Kataev, they may well apply to the search in his dreams for himself. The poem is about the spiritual renewal of a prophet whose eyes and ears are opened to the sights and sounds of good (the angels on high), and bad (the monsters in the depths of the sea), and man (the growth of the vine in the valley). The six-winged seraph who awakens the prophet then tears out his "sinful tongue" and he lies "like a corpse in the desert" (a line quoted twice by Kataev) until the voice of God commands him to arise and go forth to preach the truth to mankind:

> And God's voice called out to me:
> "Arise, Prophet, and see and hear,
> My will fulfill.
> Traverse the land and sea
> And ignite the hearts of men."

These lines, stressing the poet's duty to preach the truth, though not cited by Kataev directly, are echoed in the words of the American poet Robert Frost whom the narrator visits on his death bed. After warning mankind not to poison the wells, Frost, with the "awesome eyes of a prophet" and a "lofty prophetic" manner of speech, angrily tells the narrator: "And now you speak," [66] as if invoking him to go forth and ignite the hearts of men.

The narrator remarks that Frost seems to be looking beyond him at his "carbonized wings." The Russian woman in Los Angeles also notices the narrator's "charred wings." [67] This could be a reference to Pushkin's six-winged seraph who comes to awaken the prophet. What awakens the narrator/author is not clear. Perhaps America is a catalyst for this catharsis. The seraph is first mentioned in a passage on Houston where Kataev describes the wonders of modern technology. It is possible that the selection of Los Angeles as the home of the Russian woman has a symbolic significance. The full name of the city is *El Pueblo de Nuestra Senora La Reina de los Angeles* (City of Our Lady Queen of the Angels) and is often referred to as the City of the Angels. Whether Kataev had this in mind is difficult to say. The use of atomic war as a source of metaphor, as mentioned above, seems related to Kataev's "signals from the future." Kataev's six-winged seraph, his wings charred, seems about to be destroyed by atomic disaster, and with him, the potential greatness of mankind. The atomic disintegration theme in *The Sacred Well* thus displays a metaphysical nuance, becoming a metaphor for man's spiritual disintegration as in some of Voznesensky's beatnik poems mentioned in an earlier chapter.

The American dream concludes with the Frost scene, as the narrator finds himself unable to respond to the poet:

> What could I tell him during that last minute of our earthly meeting? I could do only one thing— loudly proclaim the name of that California ever-

green that is covered with bright red flowers in midwinter, but I had forgotten the word, the one word
that could save the world and save us all. Feeling
depressed, I remained silent but I could already hear
within myself the distant voice of another great
American poet born here in Boston more than a century before:

> And I said—"What is written, sweet sister,
> On the door of this legended tomb?"
> She replied—"Ulalume—Ulalume—
> 'Tis the vault of thy lost Ulalume!"

The quatrain is from Poe's ballad "Ulalume," also
excerpted several times by the author. The narrator finds
himself in the airplane going back to Europe, reading
the latest Paris newspapers. His final thoughts about his
voyage to America are also cryptographical:

> . . . I dozed in expectation of Europe, feeling pleas-
> antly exhausted, like a man who has dived to fearful
> depths to salvage the marble statue of a goddess and
> shot to the surface half dead from inhuman strain.
> On his outstretched palms, amid the seaweed and
> blue sand running through his fingers, he holds
> nothing more than a small time-blackened terra-
> cotta statuette of a woman, a widow, that has been
> lying on the bottom for several thousand years.

> Well, I know now this dim lake of Auber,
>   This misty mid-region of Nod [meaning Weir].

> Perhaps it is all an experiment to set up a third
> system of signals?

The allegorical nature of parts of *The Sacred Well* is alluded to again in this contrast between the idealized and the real: the image of a marble statue of a goddess that has been turned into a terracotta statuette of a widow by the waters of time. The teracotta statuette may represent the Russian woman, or even America. Or it might reveal some private area of the writer's imagination or soul. This image is difficult to identify, as are so many others. Kataev has perhaps been intentionally ambiguous, although it is curious that he refers to the statue as a widow—all of the female images in *The Sacred Well* are widows.

The couplet above is also from "Ulalume." There are three citations from this poem in the work, implying a substantial association with the thought of that poem.[68] The narrator may be equating his dream memories of America with the "misty region" of Auber and Weir/ Nod. Or it may be the "misty region" of his own soul that he is referring to. The trip to America may thus be partially an allegory of another, more personal voyage to the depths of the author's sacred well, his soul. Kataev, like Voznesensky, may be searching for "America in America, myself in myself."

The remark about attempting a third system of signals, which Kataev mentions several times in the work, is probably the best definition of the story itself. He has defined his new literary school, *mauvism,* as an attempt to unite the two dimensions of the real and the imaginary in an effort to create the only viable art. Several pages later he defines abstractionism as a subconscious attempt to create a third signal system of communication. And in the beginning of the story, he affirms that the nonexistent and the abstract belong to a new, fourth signal system, one that will replace the old system. In Kataev's description of the symbolic language of the road signs by the highway may possibly lie the best description of the author's intentions in *The Sacred Well:*

> . . . letting us know in the symbolic language of broken lines, zigzags, detours, triangles and variously colored circles and stripes, about everything that lies ahead of us, that is in the not too distant future.[69]

The author's allegorical and at times surrealistic symbols seem to be a sharp refutation of the doctrines of socialist realism which he so excelled at following for forty years. Kataev now appears to have assumed the mantle of moral philosopher.

The critical reaction to *The Sacred Well* has been extensive, but inconclusive. Perhaps out of respect for Kataev's long and distinguished career as a master of socialist realism (and perhaps out of sheer shock and confusion), almost no denouncements have been made (in comparison to the sharp attacks on Voznesensky, Nekrasov, and Yevtushenko). However, the majority of the published commentaries have been somewhat less than enthusiastic. Vladimir Dudintsev, the author of *Not By Bread Alone,* reproaches Kataev for his lack of compassion for his fellow man [70]—which seems a strange reaction to the work. The Soviet critic Eduard Skobelev finds the story in part "obscure, pretentious and artificial." [71] And three lengthy articles in the January 1968 issue of the journal *Voprosy literatury* [72] discuss *The Sacred Well* and *The Herb of Oblivion,* but do not come to any clear conclusions about these works except to note that they do differ from Kataev's earlier writings. Vladimir Gusev

summarizes these opinions with his comment that the
"peculiar laboratories" of Kataev's new literary endeavors
are not without some value. But he also goes on to say
that a whole series of such works would be a "tragedy"
for Russian literature.[75] There is no attempt in any of
these articles to analyze the *content* of *The Sacred Well*
in any depth, nor has there been any comment about
Kataev's portrait of America—other than a remark in
Dudintsev's article about the superficiality of Kataev's
observations:

> Traveling through the United States, the hero of
> the story makes many brilliant observations, but
> typically, he gives us only polaroid camera shots that
> do not present a picture of the life of the country
> and its people.

Two articles by V. Aksenev [74] and A. Morozov,[75] in
honor of Kataev on his seventieth birthday in January
1967, praise the work as a sparkling achievement for
Soviet literature. Morosov writes:

> The story is a disclosure of the creative process. In
> it Valentin Kataev has succeeded in realizing an
> idea that has long fascinated Russian writers. This
> is the wide open spaces of the unbounded novel that
> Pushkin yearned for, that which Yury Olesha ap-
> proached in his book *Not a Day Without a Line*.
> *The Sacred Well* is a story about the genesis of poetry.

Thus, the cryptography in *The Sacred Well* that we
have attempted to decipher still remains a substantial
mystery. The mosaic-like construction of the author's main

ideas, the incomplete thoughts and descriptions, the surrealistic ambiguity of many passages conceal the author's
true designs. The work gives the impression that it may
be a condensation of Kataev's personal philosophy, perhaps even of some change or revolution in his philosophy.
Someday we may understand more of his references and
allusions. Some "symbols" may be no more than ornaments
of camouflage. Some minor references may have greater
significance than is now supposed. However, the role of
America in this radical transformation of Kataev's style
seems to be a significant one. And the inclusion of a
cryptographic essay that criticizes Soviet manners in what
is mainly a travel memoir on America marks a further
step in a new tendency of Soviet writers in the 1960's
to escape from socialist realism into allegory. This last
technique is carried to perfection in some of Yevgeny
Yevtushenko's poems.

Notes

1. Isaac Babel, Yury Olesha, and Konstantin Paustovsky are other members of this informal group.
2. *Kratkaja literaturnaja ènciklopedija*, 1966, III, 438.
3. V. Kataev, *Svjatoj kolodec, Novyj mir*, V (May 1966).
4. A comparison of the original proofs of this story with the published version shows textual deletions ranging from single
words to two pages, amounting in total to about ten percent of
the original text. About half of these excisions occur in the
Georgian dream and were apparently intended to tone down
the strong anti-Stalinist expression of the satirical scenes that
were cut. Those deletions that pertain to our analysis of Kataev's American impressions will be discussed.
5. V. Kataev, *op. cit.*, 4.
6. *Ibid.*, 4–5.
7. *Ibid.*, 6.
8. *Ibid.*, 8.

9. "of Caesar" [*cezara*] in the original proofs.
10. V. Kataev, *op. cit.*, 13–14.
11. *Ibid.*, 17.
12. *Ibid.*, 20.
13. *Ibid.*, 52.
14. *Ibid.*, 40–41.
15. V. Kataev, *Trava zabven'ja, Novyj mir*, III (March 1967).
16. V. Kataev, *Novyj mir*, V (May 1966), 14.
17. *Ibid.*, 5–6.
18. *Ibid.*, 6.
19. *Ibid.*, 24–25.
20. *Ibid.*, 26.
21. *Ibid.*, 23.
22. *Ibid.*, 7.
23. *Ibid.*, 10.
24. *Ibid.*, pp. 10, 11, 20, 21, 22, 23, 24, 25, 28, 35, 62, 63, 64, 65, 66.
25. *Ibid.*, 27.
26. This impression is probably from Kataev's first visit to America in August of 1959. It is interesting to note that after a report on his first day in New York in the hot August weather, the scene shifts into the winter months. This probably is a reflection of his second longer visit in the winter and spring of 1963. The preponderance of wintry scenes, indeed the absence of any spring weather in the dream of America (as opposed to other parts of his dream), however, does suggest a conscious use of weather as a device.
27. V. Kataev, *Novyj mir,* V (May 1966), 53.
28. *Ibid.*, 49.
29. *Ibid.*, 50.
30. *Ibid.*, 28.
31. *Ibid.*, 28–29.
32. *Ibid.*, 34.
33. *Ibid.*, 35.
34. *Ibid.* (The "third" lion is a snow lion made by some children.)
35. *Ibid.*, 36.
36. A *vanka-vstanka* is a Russian doll with a weight attached to its base that causes it always to recover its standing pose.
37. V. Kataev, *Novyj mir,* V (May 1966), 54.
38. *Ibid.*, 43.
39. *Ibid.*, 60.
40. *Ibid.*, 65.
41. *Ibid.*, 58.
42. Other lines from this poem that appear in the text are: "I lay like a corpse in the wilderness," which occurs twice—once in

the Georgian dream (p. 16) and once in the American dream
(p. 30); "With fingers light as sleep he touched my eyes" opens
a paragraph describing the view from the 26th floor of his hotel
room in Houston (p. 49); and "He tore out my sinful tongue"
appears after a poignant final scene with the Russian woman
(p. 62). The six-winged seraph is mentioned on page 49 and
reappears in part toward the end of the narrative as "charred
wings" (pp. 62, 64).

43. V. Kataev, *Novyj mir*, V (May 1966), 39.
44. *Ibid.*
45. *Ibid.*, 62.
46. *Ibid.*, 58.
47. *Ibid.*, 59.
48. *Ibid.*, 62.
49. *Ibid.*, 63.
50. *Ibid.*, 64.
51. *Ibid.*, 45–46.
52. *Ibid.*, 56.
53. *Ibid.*, 45.
54. *Ibid.*, 37.
55. *Ibid.*, 37–38.
56. *Ibid.*, 44.
57. *Ibid.*
58. *Ibid.*, 66.
59. *Ibid.*
60. *Ibid.*, 3.
61. *Ibid.*, 58.
62. *Ibid.*, 22.
63. *Ibid.*, 18.
64. *Ibid.*, 41.
65. *Ibid.*, 61.
66. *Ibid.*, 64.
67. *Ibid.*, 62.
68. "Ulalume" is a mystical poem belonging to the ancient narrative genre of dialogue between body and soul, a form very popular in the Middle Ages, and also found in other American
poets (Killis Campbell, ed., *The Poems of Edgar Allan Poe*
[New York 1962] 272–273). In this poem the poet and his soul
(Psyche) wander at night amidst a dim and misty region,
". . . down by the dark tarn of Auber / In the ghoul-haunted
woodland of Weir," discussing the merits of the bright star
Astarte (Venus) which attracts the poet, but whose brilliance
is mistrusted by Psyche. The poet calms Psyche's fears and they
continue until they come to the "door of a legended tomb."

The cited quatrain follows at this point. Kataev's associations with this poem are not clear. Nor is it clear why he selected the translation of N. Čukovskij rather than the earlier and better translation of V. Brjusov. Čukovskij's arbitrary changing of Poe's "Weir" to "Nod" (the land where Cain settled after the murder of Abel) is puzzling. Perhaps Kataev wished to add this association of Nod (death, murder) to his story. He does refer to the "mark of Cain" when describing the atomic insignia on the sergeant's uniform. Perhaps he merely wished to cloud the subjective symbolism of Brjusov's interpretation of "Ulalume"—his concern with the twilight states of man's soul, as the editor of a collection of his poetry writes:

"A mournful reality instantly illuminates the memory of the unfortunate creature only at that moment when he approaches the door of the sarcophagus."—Thus does the poet Brjusov uncover the content of this poem, pointing out that "for a genuine interpretation of the poem it is necessary to recognize the 'twilight' states of our soul and their properties which have only recently become an object of scientific study." (Valerij Brjusov, *Stixotvorenija i poèmy* [Moscow 1961] 850.)

69. V. Kataev, *Novyj mir,* V (May 1966), 6.
70. V. Dudincev, *"Dve magii iskusstva," Literaturnaja gazeta,* August 13, 1966, 3.
71. Eduard Skobelev, *"Kogda menjajut serebro," Literaturnaja Rossija,* August 19, 1966, 4.
72. B. Sarnov, *"Ugl' pylajuščij i kimval brjacajuščij."*
    V. Gusev, *"Dve storony medali."*
    I. Grinberg, *"Nabljudatel'nost' ili licezrenie?"*
73. Gusev, *op. cit.,* 57–58.
74. V. Aksenev, *"Putešestvie k Kateaevu," Junost',* I (January 1967), 68–69.
75. A. Morozov, *"Povoroty vremeni," Učitel'skaja gazeta,* January 28, 1967, 4.

5.

Allegory: Yevgeny Yevtushenko, Poems

Yevgeny Yevtushenko is perhaps the most widely known contemporary Soviet poet. Born in July 1933, he is two months younger than Voznesensky but his literary career is almost a decade older. Yevtushenko's first poems appeared in a Soviet sports newspaper in 1949, and he was quite prolific during the 1950's, publishing several collections which gained him widespread recognition as a leading poet of the post-Stalin generation. His reputation has continued to grow during the sixties, and he was nominated, along with Voznesensky, for the Lenin Prize in Literature in 1966.

Yevtushenko has come close to being an ideal socialist-realist poet, lending his talents to the exposition of social and political themes as well as to the intimate lyrical expression of personal feelings. He is a gifted poet, but his dual dedication to Marx and Apollo has resulted in a somewhat uneven performance: his poems range from propagandist doggerel to truly expressive lyrics, making him a worthy descendant of the first important Soviet poet, Vladimir Mayakovsky. Yevtushenko also has done much to revive the public poetry readings in which Mayakovsky so excelled. The young poet's flamboyant style, as well as his publicized clashes with the Soviet authorities, have attracted much attention in the West where he has traveled extensively since 1960.

Yevtushenko made his first trip to the United States as a member of a group that included Voznesensky and several other Soviet writers during the spring of 1961. The trip seems to have had a profound effect on him, for soon after it a subtle but very significant change began to manifest itself in his political poems. The first evidence of this change is found in the *absence* of a barrage of anti-American poems after the trip. This is important for two reasons: first, because negative reports are expected of Soviet writers who visit America, and second, because Yevtushenko had previously excelled in the writing of anti-American poems. In marked contrast to Voznesensky's prolific cycle describing his impressions of America, Yevtushenko published only three short poems which reveal relatively little about his reaction to the United States. This paucity of comment suggests that the usually loquacious young bard may have been somewhat surprised by what he saw.

Yevtushenko launched his career as a poet with propaganda verses among which was a somewhat naïve but powerful anti-American poem, "A Boxer's Fate." [1] It relates the history of Jim, the World Boxing Champion, who is deprived of his title and livelihood in retaliation for having signed a petition against the North Atlantic Treaty, and whose sole comfort these cold, hungry days on the streets in New York is a portrait of Stalin given

him by a Russian soldier during the war. Following are
a few stanzas from the poem:

> Almost defoliating the trees
> the wind
>   scatters garbage in the squares.
> In New York—
>   the capital of profit—
> walks an unemployed boxer.
>
>   . . . .
>
> Round after round,
>   the flashing of gloves.
> The champion
>   defends himself, surprised.
> Jim
>   notices signs of exhaustion
> in the champion's movements.
>
>   . . . .
>
> Why is the famous boxer
>   wandering about the city
> shaking with hunger,
>   his teeth chattering in time
> to his steps?
> It happened thus—
> The boss
>   summoned Jim
> and asked him
>   a question.
> Losing no time
>   the boss
> asked
>   in a voice thick as syrup:
> "Is this your signature
> against the Atlantic Pact?"
>
>   . . . .

The many-time champion walks,
the square
            is grey.
Ah, no doubt
            they are ringing the bells now
in Moscow.
There people
            breathe freedom as air
under the banners
            of Stalin's inspired ideas.
There sport—
            the property of all the people—
educates men.
And Jim
            touches the cherished portrait [of Stalin],
his compass
            in the hours of ordeal and misfortune—
he sees his path:
            it lies straight,
stern and simple—
a path
      that is worth living
and fighting for!

The poem is typical propaganda verse: a hero of the masses suffers at the hands of the capitalist bosses for his proCommunist gesture, but is calmed by visions of freedom inspired by thoughts of Comrade Stalin. Yevtushenko's poetics here is rather primitive. There is not one genuine poetic image in the entire poem, which is composed of prose statements syntactically rearranged to provide occasional rhyme. There is no poetic meter. For example, here in Russian is the second stanza quoted above:

Za raundom raund,
        mel'kan'e perčatok,
čempion
    zaščiščaetsja, ošelomlennyj.
I Džim
    ustalosti otpecatok
zametil v dviženijax čempiona.

If the word order is reversed in the first and sixth lines, we have pure colloquial prose. This process may be repeated for every stanza in the poem and is a characteristic of propagandist verse. However, poetry is something more than word rearrangement, as Yevtushenko has subsequently learned.

Propagandist clichés abound in the poem: "capital of profit," "boss," "breathe freedom," "Stalin's inspired ideas," "property of the people," and so forth. Nevertheless, the poem is quite an ambitious undertaking for a sixteen-year-old, and clearly shows the potential talent that Yevtushenko was later to develop, as polemicist as well as poet.

It is this polemical spirit, however, that seems unusually silent as Yevtushenko confronts America herself. He seems a bit overwhelmed and unsure of what to say. The first poem from his American trip, "An American Nightingale," appeared in *Literaturnaja gazeta* on August 24, 1961, and was included in a collection of his poetry published in the spring of 1962.[2] The poem is an impression from the poet's visit to Cambridge. It is a weak poem, replete with oversimplification ("In the land of perlon and dacron, / and of science that has become a fetish"); awkward metaphor (a nightingale in the city of Cambridge); journalistic cliché ("half-truths and lies," "black deeds," "millions of questionnaires," "shark-like bodies of rockets"); saccharine sentimentality ("And somewhere in the heart of Russia / . . . his little Russian brother sang"); and banal observation (nightingales speak the same language; men don't understand one another).

Technically, the poem is rather loosely constructed and the poet's thoughts seem unmotivated and disconnected. For instance, the line "A bird is no load for a branch" is awkward and contributes little to the poem. The poet jumps from "the land of perlon" to "a bird on a branch," to "students on a spree," to "rockets ready for action" without much motivation or cohesion of content or of mood. Such a lack of inner consistency suggests a lack of conviction on the part of the poet as to what to say about America. The poem also seems rather drawn out and inflated in comparison with its simple presentation of the theme of nonunderstanding. Moreover, the confrontation with this nonunderstanding seems to engender strangely little regret. Hence the poet's thought appears insincere and superficial. His use of contrastive epithets such as "mournfully he sang, and happily" and unusual simile such as "the music, like a blizzard lashed" conveys an impression more of ostentatious display than of poetic depth or firm conviction, and underscores the superficiality of the poem's impressionism. At the same time, one cannot fail to mark the absence of the usual criticisms of the American scene. The students are described as happy, the weather is pleasant, and something in the surroundings apparently reaches out to the poet, calling to mind one of the tenderest images of Russian poetry, the nightingale. However untypical of the American scene this association may be, it is a sharp contrast to the "vultures of capitalism" often found in propaganda. The self-assured tone of the

young polemicist is noticeably missing here as the young
warrior [4] retreats from attack to rhetorical anecdote.

Yevtushenko recovers his balance a bit in his next
American poem, "Girl Beatnik." [5] The scene is New
York, the world is a "moralist who's been howled down."
The beatnik is pictured as running away even from
herself, finding truth only in the "twist." The fourth
stanza is broken up into two aphorisms:

> Everything strikes her as false in the world,
> everything—from the Bible to the Herald.
> The Montagues exist, and the Capulets,
> But there are no Romeos, no Juliets.

The lines are clever and striking. In Russian the words
"in the world" [na svete], "to the Herald" [do gazet],
"Capulets" [Kapuletti] and "Juliet" [Džul'ett] continue
the a b a b rhyme scheme of the rest of the poem but
also form a secondary assonantal rhyme that is nearly
identical. The imagery stresses the emptiness and confusion of the beatnik's world, where enmity exists, but
no love. Yevtushenko delights in composing such maxims,
and his poetry is full of them.

"Girl Beatnik" describes the despairing world of a
beatnik, supposedly an American, but the reference to
"spiked heels" is a curious one for American beatniks
who usually go barefoot or, at best, wear sandals. Soviet
girls, on the other hand, are quite style-conscious and
almost always wear high heels. The relative anonymity
of this beatnik, together with the absence of a comparison
to "happy" Soviet youth, distinguishes it from the didactic
mood of propagandist writings such as "A Boxer's Fate."
"Girl Beatnik" is a much better constructed poem than

"An American Nightingale," and some of its imagery is captivating. There is a striking comparison of the moon moving along its heavenly route with a drunken beatnik staggering along a well-lighted avenue. The poet cleverly reinforces this simile with the arresting epithet "milky avenue":

> Gloomy as a beatnik,
> The moon staggers in intoxication
> Along the milky avenue.

New York is also described as "beautiful but cruel." An earlier Yevtushenko would have left the "beautiful" out. The poem is a cry of despair. However, while it was supposedly written about America, the words "New York" in the first line could easily be changed to "Paris" or "Moscow" without disrupting the rest of the poem. Thus, as a concern with morality instead of ideology, it transcends political or geographical boundaries, and becomes a statement of the spiritual condition of man.

The third poem about Yevtushenko's visit to America, "Monologue of the Beatniks," [6] is quite ambiguous. Although it was written in New York, there is nothing in the text to identify it as a description of America. It, too, is a personal poem, a statement of youth—perhaps of New York, perhaps of Moscow, perhaps of the world. The poem bears signs of Yevtushenko's growing mastery: thoughts are expressed with imagination and poignance. The imagery shows a poet, not a propagandist, at work:

> The twentieth century has often fooled us.
> They've taxed us with falsehood.
> Ideas are scattered by the breath of life
> as fleetingly as dandelions.

The poet here uses assonance and alliteration with great effectiveness: *"oduračival—oduvančikov—ot dunoven'ja."* The image of ideas being scattered like dandelions is vivid and expressive, showing Yevtushenko at his creative best. The self-negating essence of irony is astutely captured in a later stanza: "Irony, you have turned from our savior into our executioner." And literary imagery is even more successfully employed in this poem than in "Girl Beatnik": "Irony, to you we've sold our soul. / receiving no Margaret in return."

The simple and direct exposition, as well as the absence of cliché and *non-sequitur,* attest to the poem's sincerity and depth, and suggest an intimate acquaintance of the poet with his theme. As such the poem may be interpreted as Yevtushenko's commentary on what he knows best: Soviet life. The ambiguity of this poem is an early example of the trend of Soviet writers in the 1960s to use their trips to America in part as camouflage for observations that do not necessarily concern America.

These three poems give some idea of the range of Yevtushenko's poetics and the long way he has come from his teen-age verses of puppet-propaganda to thoughtful reflection on the capitalist world. Upon personal acquaintance, he seems to find it not so alien nor so one-dimensional. The two beatnik poems especially show the beginnings of a change in Yevtushenko's attitude towards America, notably: the absence of political cliché, didacticism, or a denunciatory tone, the concern with moral rather than political values, and the ambiguity of his references. "An American Nightingale" and "Girl Beatnik" present us with at least a hint of admiration as well—of Cambridge and New York as beautiful cities.

Thus, though Yevtushenko's exposition of his impressions of America is rather limited on this first trip, his hesitation may be interpreted as a not unfavorable reaction to the country of capitalism. For once the young poet-polemicist seems speechless, as if his confrontation with the real America comes into conflict with the proconceived notions of propaganda. America begins to emerge as an attractive image in his poetry.

The spark of love America ignited in the heart of the young poet may be more clearly seen in "The American Cemetery," [7] a poem from his cycle of Cuban poems. Yevtushenko visited Cuba shortly after his 1961 trip to America and the memory of America seems to have haunted him. The poem describes a visit to the now uncared-for American cemetery outside of Havana. Amidst reflections on the young Americans buried in Cuban soil and the current unfriendly relations between the two countries ("Gringos are more likable under the ground," a Cuban woman tells him), the poet addresses America with the words: "I have seen you. You are great. / But are you really right in everything?" The word "great" is no small concession to America. There is no irony or sarcasm here, but a gentle, pleading tone. He uses the intimate form "thou," and the last line seems to imply that at least America is not wrong in everything. He goes on to say:

I, a Russian, would very much like
my whole life and destiny
of flights, construction, and creation
to be together, America, with you.

I would like the word "gringo"
to be cleanly erased from the dictionaries
so that all nations would respect
the graves of your sons.

Such gallantry is in pointed contrast to the contemptuous tone of propaganda. The whore of capitalism is becoming a Beautiful Lady. America the country has become America, "thou," as the poet enters a personal relationship with the America he has discovered.

This change in the poet's attitude toward America is accompanied by the beginning of some vacillation in Yevtushenko's political ideology. The teen-ager's utopia begins to show signs of fallibility. It may be significant that two outspoken poems against abuses within the Soviet Union, the famous poems "Babii Yar," decrying the persistence of antisemitism in the Soviet Union, and "The Heirs of Stalin," about the continuation of Stalinist policies by his ideological heirs, were written after his visit to America.

The year 1963 was an unhappy one for Yevtushenko. He was sharply criticized for the unauthorized publication of his autobiography in France in March and recalled home from a visit to Paris. He was sternly denounced by Khrushchev and many other officials. Mikhail Sokolov accused him of "immaturity": "Why should we send abroad young people who are far from mature either as artists or as citizens, not to mention political maturity?"[8] The April 7 issue of *Komsomolskaja pravda* devoted a whole page to correspondence condemning Yevtushenko's behavior. He was forced to cancel his projected April poetry reading tour of America and was deprived of the opportunity to travel abroad for nearly two years.

In November and December of 1966 he returned to America for a seven-week reading tour. The publication in July of a polemical poem against America's involvement in Vietnam may have seemed evidence enough of "political maturity" for the Party to let him visit America again. The poem, "A Letter to John Steinbeck." [9] marks

Yevtushenko's return to political poetry in the war against
capitalism. The poet reproaches Steinbeck for not pro-
testing the war in Vietnam:

> Is it not dreadful for you these nights
> when a pilot flies to bomb children
> perhaps
>   carrying your book about Charley?
> The winter of our discontent
>   is now.

"Charley" is Steinbeck's poodle, who accompanied the
novelist on a trip through America described in his book
Travels with Charley. The poet's description of July days
as "the winter of our discontent" (a reference to Steinbeck's novel by that name) borders on bathetic cliché.
The "poem" is versified prose rather than poetry, and is
full of the political cliché, bathos, and didacticism that
are typical of propaganda.

The first poems to appear after Yevtushenko's second
trip to America are strongly anti-American. "Slippery Ice
in New York" [10] extends the image of slippery ice in
the streets to slippery politics in a rather crude caricature:

> The warmonger
>   has slipped
> on his frozen ultra-mad dribble.
> The "peacemaker" has slipped—
>   ouch!—
> on his frozen crocodile tears!
> America has really taken a spill.
>   She's on her back.
> —America runs along the street.
> From under her hat, across her piercing blue gaze
> her Niagara-red hair flies.

America is portrayed as a Natasha Rostov (the heroine of Tolstoy's *War and Peace* and one of the most beloved feminine images in Russian literature), running through the streets, wanting only peace and a happy world "free from baseness and bombs." But someone keeps pouring icy lies beneath her feet.

The poem ends with the moralistic condescension of the skilled propagandist:

> Be more careful crossing the icy streets.
> Give me your hand,
> I'll take you across.

The poem is an apparent denunciation of the Vietnam War, and possibly the poet's "payment" for his trip to America. It is significant that the poem was printed in *Pravda* rather than in one of the literary papers. However, the strength of feeling conveyed through the consistency of the imagery does suggest some inner conviction on the part of the poet. The angry young polemicist has caught his second wind. This is Yevtushenko's most powerful anti-American poem. The crude imagery, political cliché, and contemptuous tone mark it as propaganda.

On the other hand the ending of the poem may be interpreted as the emergence of a new American image in Yevtushenko's work—an America divorced from capitalism, an innocent girl, a Natasha Rostov, to be saved by the poet. Some later poems will show that the chivalry aroused in the poet by his first visit to America (his desire to salvage the reputation of her "gringo" sons) has grown in measure with reacquaintance.

A second poem, "A Ballad of Nuggets," [11] tells the story of a drunken prospector in Alaska whose search for gold bankrupts him. The poet meets him in a bar complete with a "strip-eskimo" and hears his sad tale:

> "My whole life I searched for gold,
> > Listen, Russian!
> I once was ruddy—Here's to your health!
> > Now I'm gloomy.
> My bald skull
> > Is an airport for mosquitos."

Such amusing images break up the moralizing of the poem which exposes the ravages of gold fever. It is a poorly written poem, indicating perhaps that the poet's interest in it was not great.

His debt to the Party paid, as it were, with these two unfavorable poems about America, Yevtushenko returns to work on a cycle of verse that continues his exploration of himself and develops into allegorical commentary about the Soviet Union as well. The first of these poems, "Cemetery of Whales," [12] published two months later, is again about Alaska. The sight of whale bones on the frozen wastes calls various associations to the poet's mind. He compares the fate of the whales to the vulnerability of other giants ("Enormity commands everyone to hunt for it") whose greatness is impossible to hide ("You're broader than space! The world doesn't hold enough water / for you to dive under"). The Russian is very concise here and the images well chosen. Whom the poet is referring to becomes clear as the whale emerges as a metaphor for the great Russian writers who have been hunted down:

> A baby whale, not full-fledged,
> though evaluated as a whale,

Esenin flutters and kicks,
  hoisted high on a harpoon shaft.
The title of Whale is a bloody dignity.
  Greatness kills greatness.
Mayakovsky himself
  pounds in the lance.
        . . . . .
Without even moaning,
  gliding along the path of blood,
Pasternak with a snatch of lime
  sinks into Lethe.

These passages did not appear in the Russian version of the poem, but are in the English version that was printed in *Holiday* magazine. The poet goes on to berate the hypocrisy of the posthumous revival and mourning for the persecuted writers: "A big drive is on; / we cherish their names posthumously. / Your law is more honest, / cruel Alaska." [*Idet bol'šoj zagon, / a posle smerti —laska. / Čestnee tvoj zakon, / žestokaja Aljaska.*] Again the conciseness of the Russian is very forceful, due to the crisp iambic trimeter and the dramatic assonance of the rhyme. The poet concludes that life is better among the Eskimos, who have some "tact" and sense of decency before the dead.

"Cemetery of Whales" is a powerfully written poem that points toward the beginning of an allegorical tendency in Yevtushenko's poems about America. There is little ambiguity here—the poet himself defines his symbols quite clearly. Later poems become more cryptographical as the poet finds his candor ill rewarded (the censoring of the cited passages from the Russian version).

There is an especially delightful image in the beginning of the poem describing an old hunchbacked Eskimo

huddling like a question mark between the "parentheses"
of the whale bones.

The latest poems from Yevtushenko's new American
cycle, which appeared in January 1968 in the journal
Znamja, are highly cryptographical. Alaska again serves
as background for "Monologue of a Fox on an Alaskan
Fur Farm," [13] a poem which may be interpreted as an
allegory of the poet in Russia. The poem opens as follows:

> I am a blue fox on a grey farm.
> Condemned to slaughter by my color
> behind this gnawproof wire screen,
> I find no comfort in being blue.

The poet realizes how different he is from everyone
around him, and that his nonconformity dooms him to
early extinction. He yearns for his freedom, but finds
he cannot live outside his cage: "A child of captivity
is too weak for freedom./ He who's conceived in a cage
will cry for a cage." The poet's agonizing dilemma is
repeated again in the succeeding lines:

> Horrified, I understood how much I love
> that cage, where they hide me behind a screen,
> and the fur farm—my motherland.

"Motherland" is a telling metaphor here, and one that
strongly alludes to allegory. The poet earlier refers to
his cage as his "native Dachau," a terror-striking image.
The identification of the fox with the poet may also be
suggested in the line: "My mother and father did not
love one another." Yevtushenko's parents were divorced
when he was quite young.

The doomed fox comments with irony on the farm improvements—they kill by electrocution now instead of suffocation. And he accepts his fate with almost chilling equanimity:

> I would like to be naïve, like my father,
> but I was born in captivity: I am not he.
> The one who feeds me will betray me.
> The one who pets me will kill me.

The poet's imagery in these American poems is endlessly varied and thought-provoking. In another stanza of the Alaskan dog poem the agony of the poet's position is poignantly conveyed:

> Alaska's snowdrifts towered all around,
> and I desperately capered, diseased,
> and freedom danced a Twist inside my lungs
> with the stars I had swallowed.

Later in the poem, Yevtushenko breaks from the narrative about the caged fox to an emotional outpouring to America:

> In you, Alaska, I howled in lost despair.
> In prison now, I am howling in despair.
> My America, I am lost,
> but who hasn't gotten lost in you?

"In prison now" would seem to refer to the Soviet Union since it is contrasted to Alaska.

Significantly enough America seems to have become

a personified female figure whom the poet treats with great tenderness and affection and to whom he reaches out in times of despair. This has formerly been a role reserved for Russia. That Yevtushenko, like Voznesensky, is strongly attracted to the capitalist beauty cannot be doubted. There is something in America with which both poets strongly identify. For Yevtushenko capitalist America becomes "my America," right beside "my Russia." America has not supplanted Russia in the poet's soul—he remains deeply attached to his motherland. But if Russia is his mother, his stern parent, America is perhaps his sister, his understanding friend. She is no longer the cause of all the miseries of the world, as Communist propaganda suggests, but a covictim of the suffocating times. The poet would like to save her as well as himself, but he does not know how.

In another poem from his cycle, "Monologue of an American Poet," [14] he continues his despairing cry to America:

America, look,
I'm finished,
I'm finished,
I'm finished.

He compares himself to a ship that smells of doom, and cries that his friends are deserting him as rats abandon a sinking ship. The poem, supposedly the monologue of an American poet, is also probably an allegorical expression of the poet who wrote it. It is very similar, in mood and tone, to Voznesensky's "Monologue with Footnotes," and like the latter, is dedicated to the American poet, Robert Lowell. In Voznesensky's poem San Francisco is the

Beautiful Lady ("I love you, San Francisco. . . . Sigh for me,
San Francisco.") Both poems are laments of poets en-
circled by darkness.[15] The "leaden skies" of New York
(Moscow?) circle above Yevtushenko's poet like a black
vulture. Voznesensky's "airplane," which may be con-
strued as a metaphor for the poet's soul, flies through
darkness: "Whither in such darkness, my poor little
plane?"

A presentiment of his own doom seems to beshadow
the poet in many of his poems along with a feeling of
hopelessness and despair. A third poem, "Monologue of
a Broadway Actress," [16] decries the lack of "roles":

> Said an actress from Broadway,
>   devastated as ancient Troy:
> "There is no role
> no role
>   to extract all my tears,
> no role
>   to turn my soul inside out.
>
>   .   .   .   .   .
>
> No role
>   no role
> amid hundreds of roles!
> We are drowning in rolelessness.
>
>   .   .   .   .   .
>
> Yes, there are
>   road companies.
> Yes, there is
>   comfort.
> They've removed the roles
> And substituted bit parts.

The references to "comfort" and "bit parts" allude
to an allegorical level for the poem. The poet may be

tired of playing his assigned role—a bit part in the world of politics with his propaganda poems for which he is rewarded with a comfortable life. He seeks the true poet's immortal role:

Without a role life is but decay.
We are all geniuses in the womb,
but potential geniuses perish
from the lack of potential roles.
Without demanding anybody's blood,
I
    demand
        a role!

The poem is constructed around the word "role" which is repeated very effectively. The lines referring to farmers and workers being without "roles," the references to Hiroshima, the "perishing of the innocent," and "all our pain" ascribe a metaphysical level to the role demanded by the actress (or by the poet), perhaps the role of finding an answer for the world's seemingly insurmountable problems—the role of honesty and meaningfulness. If so, then the implication is that Communism does not offer this role.

The poem is strongly reminiscent of Voznesensky's "Monologue of Marilyn Monroe," in form (repetition of a key word), outer theme (monologue of an American actress), and content (the despairing cry for a meaningful existence). "Monologue of a Broadway Actress" is by no means an imitation of Voznesensky's poem—it has its own strong individuality—but it may well have been inspired by the latter.

Still another poem, "Monologue of an American Wanderer," [17] continues the intimate relationship of the

poet with America. Again as with a beloved, the poet
talks quietly with America in the park at night. The
impressionism of the poem is striking:

> I talked with my footsteps—
> Unlike words, they do not lie—
> And she answered me with circles
> Dead leaves uttered falling onto a pond.

The poem is a long impressionistic description of
snow falling in Central Park at night. This is in itself
almost a rebuke to the favored Soviet presentation of
Central Park as a symbol of crime in America. Yevtushenko
wanders unmolested through the peace of a snowy white
night in silent communion with America. America is not
an adversary, but the poet's companion. The first stanza
clearly disassociates the poem from politics:

> At night, in New York's Central Park,
> chilled thoroughly and belonging to no one,
> I talked quietly with America:
> both of us were tired of speeches.

Walking past the zoo he finally comes to an area by the
children's zoo marked "Place for Lost Children":

> At night, beneath this snowfall,
> its whispered secret having made us one,
> America and I sat down together
> in the place for lost children.

The theme of lostness is poignantly conveyed in another stanza describing the onlooking walruses as "lost

children of the sea" who take pity on people, the "lost children of the earth."

The suffocating world is portrayed again in "Smog." [18] The smog of New York soon becomes a metaphor for the state of the world:

> . . . people have been cruelly deceived,
> the earth has been set on false whales.
> And all of mankind
> is overfatigued
> from strain.

The whale image is a reference to the Slavic folk legend that describes the world as supported on the backs of three whales. The implication here is that the whales, or philosophies, that currently support the world, including Communism, are false. The falsehood of the world seems to surround the poet here, recalling the disillusion of "Girl Beatnik." Smog, thus, becomes a metaphor for polluted ethics and morals as well:

> All the false ideas,
>   false morality,
> fuming so many years,
>   have soiled the sky.
> The sky sends this filth back.

Above the smog and fumes the poet hears the voice of Whitman (reminiscent of Frost's advice to Kataev) who urges mankind to breathe deeply in one collective breath to remove the smog from the air. The poet concludes:

And I felt the epoch
        standing still and awaiting
our common deep breath
        like an ecumenical advance.

A deep breath has replaced the inspiration of Lenin as
the purgative of the world's decay. Not the "Communist
revolution" but an "ecumenical advance" is needed. This
is a sharp departure from Communism's uncompromising
ideological battle with the capitalist world. Here the
poet inhabits the realm of morality, not of politics.

The sixth poem in this series of American poems,
"Monologue of a Teen-ager," [19] is a short but startling
synopsis of the poet's plight:

Something is forbidden me
by myself or by someone,
I wander, my hat over my eyes,
my insides chafing.

I am not allowed! This is alien to me.
Everywhere, tormenting and irritating,
events and feelings are in conflict.
Written on their brows: "Not about us."

New York, I climb aboard your autobus
and look longingly at the world,
as a drunkard who's taken Antabuse
looks longingly through the tavern window.

But should I forget
and do as I wish,
for breaking this ban
I'll pay with my life.

This poem lends itself to a cryptographical allusion to forbidden themes in Yevtushenko's poetry—it certainly does not describe the undisciplined American teen-ager of the 1960's. "About us—forbidden!" [*O nas—nel'zja*] probably refers to his criticisms of the Soviet Union. The last stanza repeats the theme of execution so candidly stated in the poem about the Alaskan dog. The terseness of the Russian here is equally chilling:

> *I esli ja zabudu èto*
> *i esli budu, kak xoču,*
> *za narušenie zapreta*
> *svoeju žizn'ju zaplaču.*

Artistically, these last six poems about America are among the best of Yevtushenko's creative work. The imagery is concise and powerful. The precise employment of assonances, internal rhymes, and unusual associations marks a profound maturation of his poetics. The inner consistency and simplicity of theme attest to the poet's sincerity and depth of conviction. The strong feelings Yevtushenko displays toward America indicate a dissolving of the ideological blueprint and the search for a moral philosophy that will reconcile his deep love of his own country with his deep attraction for America. The confusion of his first poems about America has given way to despair over his own purposelessness, and disenchantment with the morality of the world on both sides of the globe. A strong desire to save the world alternates with ' cynicism over its seemingly hopeless state.

The poet's apparent disenchantment with the land of the commissars reaches its most forcible expression in an allegorical poem published in June 1968, "By the

Forgotten Roman Way." [20] The poem contains the reflections of the poet as he stands by an ancient Roman
road near Damascus. Thinking about the road built on
the blood of its slave labor, and analyzing the arguments
advanced over the question of the road's guilt for this
bloodletting, the poet concludes that the road cannot be
absolved of blame:

> But generations of wild grass
> have handily settled the score.
> Having given birth to crimes,
> the road itself is criminal.

The prophetic thoughts of an Arab slave working
on the road are recalled by the poet. In answer to the
architect's arrogant assertion that the Empire and the
road will live forever, the slave reflects that having forgotten God, both the builders and the road will perish:

> Thinking only about matter,
> you have forgotten God.
> This means that you will die,
> and the road will die.

The thought that a road that forgets God will in turn
be forgotten by Him is fully developed at the end of
the poem:

> Thus I mused on a road
> now closed to traffic,
> on a road that forgot about God
> and is now forgotten by God.

Again the conciseness of the Russian makes it difficult to convey the forcefulness of the original in translation. The poet may be referring here to the road of Communism. The ambiguity of the poem is so complete that there are almost no concrete clues toward identifying the allegory. Only in relation to some of his other poems, some explicit, such as "Babii Yar," "The Heirs of Stalin," and "The Cemetery of Whales," and some cryptographical, such as "The Alaskan Fox" and "Monologue of a Teenager," does any definite evidence emerge to identify the Roman road as an allegory of the road to Communism, whose bloodletting Yevtushenko has persistently deplored in the poems mentioned. That he is thinking beyond merely the Roman road is emphasized by the penultimate stanza warning that a similar fate will befall all "executioner-roads."

A profound evolution seems to have taken place during the past twenty years in Yevtushenko's ideology— from a blind faith in Stalin's road to Communism ("a path that is worth living and fighting for") to a deep revulsion over the blood-covered stones of that road. An atheistic political ideology seems to have been replaced by a Christian moral concern for man as something more than matter. In another poem, dedicated to the memory of Robert Kennedy and entitled "The Mark of Cain," [21] Yevtushenko handles the theme of fratricide in biblical imagery. He also extends the definition of murder beyond physical extinction to spiritual corruption: "corruption of souls is bloodless—but it is fratricide!"

Yevtushenko also wrote some propaganda poems for *Pravda* in June: "Freedom to Kill," [22] about Kennedy's murder, and "Monologue of Doctor Spock," [23] about the trial of Spock. Another propaganda poem, "Ballad of Raised Fists," [24] was dedicated to the two Negro athletes

who raised their fists at the Olympics in the fall of 1968.
The poet thus has not completely ceased his attacks on
America—these poems are typical of his propagandist
verses—but their comparative weakness, both in imagery
and in structure, suggest that they may have been motivated by a desire on the part of the poet to save his
skin for a while longer. Or they may be a reflection of
the poet's own dual nature. Yevtushenko seems to describe his own nature best in a poem entitled "Yes and
No," [25] published in 1965:

> I am like a train,
> > shuttling for years
> between the city of "Yes"
> > and the city of "No."
> My nerves are strained
> > like telephone wires
> between the city of "No"
> > and the city of "Yes."

His indecision may be further elucidated in the following lines from a recent untitled poem: [26]

> There is strength in uncertainty
> when you venture not to go
> along a false path
> where will o' the wisps lie ahead.

Despite his propagandist verses, Yevtushenko has
apparently reserved a special place in his heart for America, a feeling that comes out strongly in the poems we
have examined. As the soul of America offers him solace

and companionship, so the form of America offers him allegorical camouflage for the outpourings of his own soul. He says that he risks his life to do so, and he may well be right. With the fervor of a romantic idealist he seeks to return the "spirit of the Elbe" to the relationship between America and the Soviet Union. In the preface to a collection of his poetry in English, Yevtushenko writes:

> Sometime in 1945, Russian and American soldiers met on the River Elbe. As they sailed to meet each other over its spring waters, they waved weapons and flasks of whiskey and vodka.
> They embraced, drank, sang, fired into the air, and showed each other tattered photographs of their sweethearts, wives and children.
> . . . the spirit of the Elbe lives on in the hearts of our peoples, for all people have the same enemies —in peace and in war: militarists, spies, exploiters, nationalists, stiflers of honor, goodness and justice. Let these feelings toward our common enemies create for us a common goal, as once it did on the River Elbe.[27]

In another poem published in *Holiday,* but not yet published in Russian, Yevtushenko returns to this theme of the spirit of the Elbe. The poem, "In a Steelworker's Home," [28] describes the poet's love for America:

> I love America,
>   the America who now
> sits with me in the prefab ranchhouse
> of a steelworker.

Here the poet returns to a collective America, the country
of the working man, rather than "America, thou," but
he is seeking coexistence, he is not proselytizing Communist ideology: "There are no governments between
us now. / Our invisible government / has been chosen by
us wordlessly."

In that same preface mentioned above the poet
continues:

> Differences in political systems should not pre-
> vent our peoples living in peace and friendship, for
> in our friendship lies the only possibility of achiev-
> ing a peaceful future for our children.
>
>   .   .   .   .   .
>
> In the final analysis, humanity has only two ways
> out—either universal destruction or universal brother-
> hood. Both right-wing and left-wing phrases about
> the impossibility of peaceful coexistence of countries
> with different systems are criminal, even if they arise
> simply out of thoughtlessness.[29]

The recurrent theme of pollution is strongly expressed in the poem:

> For twenty years they have polluted the Elbe.
> They've dumped so much sewage in her—
> the backwaters of falsehood,
>   our era's super-cesspools:
> Newspapers soaked in poison,
>   dregs of inflammatory speeches

And the theme of understanding is more funda-
mentally expressed here than in "An American Nightingale":

Oh, when
   will we understand each other
as vodka and whiskey—
   straight!—without translation
understood
   each other perfectly,
      goddammit
on the waters where victory met victory!

The poet ends on a note of optimistic hope that the spirit of the Elbe will succeed in reuniting America and Russia. He also reaffirms his love for America—

I love America,
   the America who now,
snuggled in her crib, wiggles her delicate toes;
her slender feet shine for us, the disenchanted, the
   weary—

and again identifies himself with "the disenchanted, the weary" for whom America shines.

Yevtushenko thus echoes Nekrasov's strong urgings for reconciliation, expands Voznesensky's feelings of personal attachment for America, and develops Kataev's allegory to a perfected form. Politics give way to a humanistic concern for the welfare of all mankind—not just the welfare of man's body, but the welfare of his soul. There are strong hints of a re-Christianization of Russian thought in the later poems of Yevgeny Yevtushenko. He seems to be striving to assume the prerevolutionary role of the poet in Russia as the *moral* conscience of his people. He believes the role of the artist in reconciling the peoples of the world to be a prime one:

. . . a tremendous part in strengthening friendship between our peoples must be played by art, whose eternal role is the uniting of human hearts in the name of goodness and justice.[30]

America appears to have played a major role in this conversion.

Notes

1. Y. Yevtushenko, "Sud'ba boksera," Sovetskij sport, November 17, 1949, 4.
2. Y. Yevtushenko, "Amerikanskij solovej," Vzmax ruki (Moscow 1962), 38–39.
3. See Andrei Sinyavsky's interesting article discussing the superficialities of Yevtushenko's style: "On Evtushenko," trans. Henry Gifford, Encounter, IV (April 1967), 33–43.
4. Yevtushenko compares the poet to a soldier in his poem "Poetry," written about the same time as his American poems: "Poetry is savage war. . . . The poet is a soldier." Nežnost' (Moscow 1962), 56–58.
5. Y. Yevtushenko, "Bitnica," ibid., 48–49.
6. Y. Yevtushenko, "Monolog bitnikov," ibid., 50–51.
7. Y. Yevtushenko, "Amerikanskoe kladbišče," ibid., 137–140.
8. M. Sokolov, Speech before the Writers' Union, Literaturnaja gazeta, April 2, 1963, 3.
9. Y. Yevtushenko, "Pis'mo Džonu Stejnbeku," Literaturnaja gazeta, July 7, 1966, 4.
10. Y. Yevtushenko, "Gololed v N'ju-Jorke," Pravda, February 12, 1967, 3.
11. Y. Yevtushenko, Ballada o samorodkax," ibid.
12. Y. Yevtushenko, "Na kladbišče kitov," Moskva (March 1967), 156. English translation by John Updike and Albert C. Todd in Holiday, November, 1968, 42.
13. Y. Yevtushenko, "Monolog pesca na aljaskinskoj zveroferme," Znamja, I (January 1968), 54–56. English translation by Updike and Todd, op. cit., 40.
14. Y. Yevtushenko, "Monolog amerikanskogo poèta," Znamja, I (January 1968), 57–58.

15. This image of darkness may be related to the symbol of darkness in M. Bulgakov's novel, *The Master and Margarita,* the symbol discussed by L. Rzhevsky in *"Pilatov grex: Tajnopis' v romane M. Bulgakova, 'Master i Margarita,'* Novyj zurnal, No. 90 (March 1968).

16. Y. Yevtushenko, *"Monolog brodvejskoj aktrisy,"* Znamja, I (January 1968), 56–57.

17. Y. Yevtushenko, *"Monolog amerikanskogo brodjagi,"* ibid., 60–61. English translation as "New York Elegy" by Updike and Todd, *op. cit.*

18. Y. Yevtushenko, *"Smog,"* Znamja, I (January 1968), 52–54.

19. Y. Yevtushenko, *"Monolog tinejdžera,"* ibid., 59.

20. Y. Yevtushenko, *"U rimskoj zabytoj dorogi,"* Ogonek, No. 27 (June 29, 1968), 13.

21. Y. Yevtushenko, *"Kainova pečat',"* ibid., 12.

22. Y. Yevtushenko, *"Svoboda ubivat',"* Pravda, June 7, 1968, 3.

23. Y. Yevtushenko, *"Monolog doktora Spoka,"* Pravda, June 17, 1968, 5.

24. Y. Yevtushenko, *"Ballada o podnjatyx kulakax,"* Sovetskij sport, October 22, 1968, 3.

25. Y. Yevtushenko, *" 'Da' i 'net,' "* Junost', VI (June 1965), 62–63.

26. Y. Yevtushenko, *"Prokljat'e veka—eto speška . . ."* Ogonek, No. 27 (June 29, 1968), 12.

27. *Yevtushenko Poems,* trans. by Herbert Marshall (New York 1966), 7.

28. Y. Yevtushenko, *"In a Steelworker's Home,"* trans. by Updike and Todd, *op. cit.,* 38.

29. Marshall, *op. cit.,* 7–8.

30. *Ibid.,* 8.

Conclusion

The 1960s have witnessed a rediscovery of America by four leading Soviet poets and writers who visited the United States during this time. The harsh tone of earlier literary works on America has given way in the writings of Voznesensky, Nekrasov, Kataev, and Yevtushenko, if not to praise of the American way of life, at least to sympathy, ambivalent respect, and a striking diminution of propagandist attack. Rejecting the prevailing ideological caricature of the capitalist queen, they seek an acquaintance with her soul. Some of them openly admire much of what they see, and feel a deep sense of shame for the crude behavior of certain of their compatriots. Victor Nekrasov and Valentin Kataev seems to be especially sensitive on this point. Keenly aware of the tensions in the world today and of man's capacity for self-destruction, they reach out in friendship to America despite the sharp denunciations their gestures have provoked from the Soviet leadership. As human beings they are rebelling against the climate of hate fostered by the ideological war and are seeking the warmth of understanding and of spiritual brotherhood.

Concurrent with this new "discovery of America" is a cautious depiction of Soviet fallibility, a rebellion against the utopian myth of Communism, a dissatisfaction with the strait jacket of socialist realism, and a re-awakening awareness of the spiritual nature of man. Some of the weaknesses within Soviet society, particularly the lack of personal freedom and purges of innocent people, seem to be touching chords of revulsion in these writers. They are struggling to free literature from politics, and are eager to reassume the prerevolutionary role of the Russian writer as the voice of his nation's conscience.

The deep and sincere faith in Communism expressed by Gorky, Mayakovsky, and Ilf and Petrov is noticeably missing in these writers' most recent works. This lapse of faith is most strongly felt in the younger poets Vozne-senky and Yevtushenko. Raised under the ideals of Communism, they are beginning to question the gap between the promise and the performance, especially after viewing the outside world and comparing its performance with the dour predictions of their propaganda. They seem to be aware, as was Pilnyak, of the contemporary game of chess being played with man, a match not merely between capitalism and Communism, but between Good and Evil, between forces that transcend political ideologies.

A rediscovery of America and a reassessment of the Soviet Union have been accompanied by a third explora-tion for these four authors, perhaps the most important one for each, a voyage into the depths of his own soul. The old socialist-realist writer, Valentin Kataev, and the young poet-warrior, Yevgeny Yevtushenko, especially seem to be undergoing profound catharses, as individuals as well as writers.

There are many indications in these writings that America has played a decisive role in this personal and artistic rebirth, both as an object of respectful attention and exploration, and as a camouflage for cryptographical themes about the Soviet Union. As artists, these four writers seem to be rebelling against the narrow confines of socialist realism in a search for freedom of expression, through cryptography where necessary. No doubt some of the new forms may be a result of experimentation with stylistic devices, especially in the poems of Andrei Voznesensky. But at least as many seem to be attempts to disguise the forbidden content contained in the works. Because themes of reconciliation and reassessment are prohibited under socialist realism, these writers are devising new means of literary expression that range from digression to allegory. A surrealism new to Soviet literature is emerging, a cryptographical style strangely similar to the "phantasmagoric art" predicted by the now incarcerated critic and writer, Abram Tertz, in his essay, *On Socialist Realism:*

> Right now I put my hope in a phantasmagoric art, with hypotheses instead of a Purpose, an art in which the grotesque will replace realistic descriptions of ordinary life. Such an art corresponds best to the spirit of our time. May the fantastic imagery of Hoffmann and Dostoevsky, of Goya, Chagall and Mayakovsky (the most socialist realist of all) and of many other realists and nonrealists teach us how to be truthful with the aid of the absurd and the fantastic.
>
> Having lost our faith, we have not lost our enthusiasm about the metamorphoses of God that take place before our very eyes, the miraculous transformations of His entrails and His cerebral convolutions. We don't know where to go; but, realizing

that there is nothing to be done about it, we start to think, to set riddles, to make assumptions. We may thus invent something marvelous? Perhaps; but it will no longer be socialist realism.[1]

Notes

1. A. Tertz, *On Socialist Realism* (New York 1960), 94–95. English translation by George Dennis.

A Selected Bibliography

Primary Sources

Evtušenko, Evgenij. "America and I Sat Down Together," Trans. John Updike and Albert C. Todd, *Holiday*, November 1968, 38-43.

——. *"Ballada o podnjatyx kulakax,"* Sovetskij sport, October 22, 1968, p. 3.

——. " 'Da' i 'net'," *Junost'*, VI (June 1965), 62-63.

——. *"Monolog doktora Spoka,"* Pravda, June 17, 1968, p. 5.

——. *"Na kladbišče kitov,"* Moskva, III (March 1967), 156.

——. *Nežnost'*. Moscow 1962.

——. *"Novye stixi,"* Ogonek, No. 27 (June 29, 1968), 12-13.

——. *"Novye stixi,"* Pravda, February 12, 1967, p. 3.

——. *"Novye stixi iz amerikanskoj tetradi,"* Znamja, I (January 1968), 52-61.

——. *"Pis'mo Džonu Stejnbeku,"* Literaturnaja gazeta, July 7, 1966, p. 4.

———. "Sud'ba boksera," *Sovetskij sport,* November 17, 1949, p. 4.

———. "Svoboda ubivat'," *Pravda,* June 7, 1968, p. 3.

———. "The Spirit of Elbe: To My American Readers," *Yevtushenko Poems,* Trans. Herbert Marshall, New York 1966, 7-12.

———. *Vzmax ruki.* Moscow 1962.

Gor'kij, Maxim. *Pis'ma k E.P. Peškovoj, 1895-1906.* Arxiv A.M. Gor'kogo, V, Moscow 1955.

———. *Sobranie sočinenij v 18 tomax.* Moscow 1960-63.

———. *Sobranie sočinenij v 30 tomax.* Moscow 1949-56.

———. "The City of Mammon: My Impressions of America," *Appleton's Magazine* (New York), VII (August 1906), 177-182.

Il'f, Ilja and Petrov, Evgenij. *Sobranie sočinenij v 5 tomax.* Moscow 1961.

Kataev, Valentin. "Svjatoj kolodec," *Novyj mir,* V (May 1966) 3-66.

———. "Trava zabven'ja," *Novyj mir,* III (March 1967), 3-129.

Majakovskij, Vladimir. *Ob Amerike.* Moscow 1952.

———. *Sobranie Sočinenij v 8 tomax.* Moscow 1968.

Nekrasov, Viktor. "Deduška i vnuček," *Novyj mir,* IX (September 1968), 42-65.

———. "Pervoe znakomstvo," *Novyj mir,* VII, VIII (July, August 1958), 142-181, 123-159.

———. "Po obe storony okeana," *Novyj mir,* XI, XII (November, December 1962), 112-148, 110-152.

———. *Putešestvija v raznyx izmerenijax.* Moscow 1967.

Pil'njak, Boris. *O-kèj, amerikanskij roman.* Moscow 1933.

Voznesenskij, Andrej. *Antimiry.* Moscow 1964.

———. *Axillesovo serdce.* Moscow 1966.

———. "Monolog s primečanijami," *Izvestia,* January 18, 1967, p. 4.

———. *Mozajka.* Moscow 1960.

————. "Novye stixi," Komsomolskaja Pravda, June 16, 1968, p. 3.

————. Treugol'naja gruša, Moscow 1962.

————. "Zabastovka striptiza," Literaturnaja gazeta, March 22, 1967, p. 14.

Secondary Sources

Aksenov, Vasilij. "Putešestvie k Kataevu," Junost', I (January 1967), 68-69.

"A Talk With Andrei Voznesensky," (Transcript of TV Conversation), Atlantic, July 1966, 49-52.

Banta, Lucille. "A Chat With Voznesensky," American Dialogue, VI (November-December 1966), 10-14.

Barghoorn, Frederick C. Politics in the U.S.S.R. Boston 1966.

————. Soviet Foreign Policy. Princeton 1964.

————. The Soviet Image of the United States. New York 1950.

Blake, Patricia (ed.). The Bedbug and Selected Poetry. New York 1960.

———— and Max Hayward. (ed.) Antiworlds. New York 1966.

Borland, Harriet. Soviet Theory and Practice During the First Five-Year Plan, 1928-32. New York 1950.

Brown, Deming. Soviet Attitudes Toward American Writing. Princeton 1962.

Brown, Edward J. The Proletarian Episode in Russian Literature, 1929-1932. New York 1953.

Burenin, Nikolaj. "Poezdka A.M. Gor'kogo v Ameriku," Novyj mir, VI (June 1940), 192-201.

Carlisle, Olga. "A Rider On the New Wave of Russian Poets," New York Times Book Review, October 13, 1963, p. 54.

Dudincev, Vladimir. *"Dve magii iskusstva,"* *Literturnaja gazeta,* August 13, 1966, p. 3.

"Gorky's First Impressions Revised," (editorial), *The Independent* (New York), LXI, No. 3008, July 26, 1906, p. 2.

Grinberg, I. *"Nabljudatel'nost' ili licezrenie?"* *Voprosy literatury,* I (January 1968), 61-77.

Gronskij, I. M. Speech before Second Plenary Session of the Organization Committee of Writers' Union. *Novyj mir,* II (February 1933), 248-260.

Gusev, Vladimir. *"Dve storony medali,"* *Voprosy literatury.* I (January 1968), 50-60.

Handler, M. S. "Soviet Poet Sees Literary Rebirth," *New York Times,* April 30, 1967, p. 80.

Holtzman, Filia. "A Mission That Failed: Gor'kij in America," *The Slavic and East European Journal,* VI, 3 (Fall 1962), 227-235.

Inkeles, Alex. *Public Opinion in Soviet Russia.* Cambridge 1950.

Istorija russkoj sovetskoj literatury (3 vols). Moscow 1958-61.

Kaun, Alexander. *Maxim Gorky and his Russia.* New York 1931.

Kratkaja literaturnaja ènciklopedija. (5 vols to date). Moscow 1962-

Laserson, Max M. *The American Impact on Russia, 1784-1917.* New York 1950.

Literaturnaja ènciklopedija (11 vols). Moscow 1929-39.

Ljaskovskij, Aleksandr. *Martirolog russkix pisatelej* (2 vols). Munich 1963.

Magidoff, Robert. "American Literature in Russia," *Saturday Review,* November 2, 1946, pp. 9-11, 45-46.

Marshall, Herbert (trans.). *Voznesensky: Selected Poems.* New York 1966.

————. *Yevtushenko Poems.* New York 1966.

Morozov, A. *"Povoroty vremeni,"* *Učitel'skaja gazeta,* January 28, 1967, p. 4.

Nazarenko, V. *"Nastuplenie ili otstuplenie?"* *Zvezda,* VII (July 1962), 181-188.

New York American. April-October 1906.

New York Tribune. April-October 1906.

Nilsson, Nils Åke. *"Usad'ba noč'ju, čingisxan',* Verbs Derived from Personal Names as a Means of Expression in Literary Russian," *Lingua Viget* (Festschrift in Honor of V. Kiparsky), Helsinki 1964, 97-101.

Reavey, George (trans.). *The New Russian Poets, 1953 to 1966.* New York 1966.

————. *The Poetry of Yevgeny Yevtushenko.* New York 1965.

Rodičev, Nikolaj. *"O sovremennosti v stixax,"* *Literatura i žizn',* No. 49 (April 25, 1962), 3.

Rževskij, Leonid. *"Pilatov grex: tajnopis' v romane M. Bulgakova, 'Master i Margarita',"* *Novyj žurnal,* No. 90 (March 1968), 60-80. Reprinted in L. Rževskij, *Pročten'e tvorčeskogo slova,* New York 1970.

Sarnov, V. *"Ugl' pylajuščij i kimval brjasajuščij,"* *Voprosy literatury,* I (January 1968), 21-49.

Seghers, Pierre (ed.). *The Art of Painting in the Twentieth Century.* New York 1965.

Simmons, Ernest J. *Through the Glass of Soviet Literature.* New York 1953.

Sinyavsky, Andrei. "On Evtushenko," *Encounter,* IV (April 1967), 33-43.

Sjeklocha, Paul and Mead, Igor. *Unofficial Art in the Soviet Union.* Berkeley 1967.

Skobelev, Èduard. *"Kogda menjajut serebro,"* *Literaturnaja Rossija,* August 19, 1966, p. 4.

Sokolov, Mixail. Speech before the Writers' Union. *Literaturnaja gazeta,* April 2, 1963, p. 3.

Swayze, Harold. *Political Control of Literature in the U.S.S.R., 1946-1959.* Cambridge 1962.

Tertz, Abram. *On Socialist Realism* (trans. George Dennis). New York 1960.

"*Turist s trostočkoj,*" *Izvestia,* January 20, 1963, p. 5.

Viereck, Peter. "The Mob Within the Heart: A New Russian Revolution," *Tri-Quarterly,* Spring 1965, 7-43.

The World (New York). April-October 1906.

Xruščev, Nikolaj S. Speech before Writers' Union on March 8. *Pravda,* March 10, 1963, pp. 1-4.

Index

Aesopian, 50, 51, 76
Anacin, 103
Aksenov, V., 167
Amfiteatrov, A. V., 11

Banta, Lucille, 78
Barghoorn, Frederick C., xiii, 115
Blake, Patricia, 43
Bulgakov, Mikhail, xi, xii, 76, 204

Carlisle, Olga, 57
Coca-Cola, 41, 56, 59, 103
Cooper, James Fenimore, ix, 90, 91
Cubism, 77

Dali, Salvador, 105-106
Dennis, George, 208
Dudintsev, V., 166, 167

Frost, Robert, 150, 151, 162-163, 194
    "The Lesson for Today," 151

Gogol, Nikolai V., 121, 122, 143, 144
Gorky, Maxim, x, xiii, 3, 4-12, 13, 22, 23, 25, 29, 38, 40, 134, 135, 206
    "The City of Mammon," 6
    "The City of the Yellow Devil," 4-12, 22, 134, 142
    Mother, 12
Grandma Moses, 107
Gronsky, I. M., 23-24, 29
Gusev, Vladimir, 166-167

Highet, Gilbert, 45
Holtzman, Filia, 42

Ilf, Ilya and Evgeny Petrov, xiii, 3-4, 29, 30-44, 51, 143, 206
    "Columbus Moors to the Shore," 30, 41
    One-Storied America, 30-44
    "Tonya," 30, 38-40
Izvestia, 81, 86

Kataev, Valentin, xi, xii, 58, 59, 61, 64, 76, 80, 115, 117-171, 202, 205-206
  The Herb of Oblivion, 128
  Lonely White Sail, 117
  The Sacred Well, 59, 61, 117-171
  Time, Forward!, 117
  Waves of the Black Sea, 117
Khlebnikov, V., 19
Khrushchev, Nikolai S., x, xi, 64-65, 81, 143, 183

Ladyzhnikov, I. P., 11
Lowell, Robert, 71, 190

Magidoff, Robert, v, xiii
Mandelstam, Osip, 125, 126
Marshall, Herbert, 204
Mauvism, 127, 128, 165
Mayakovsky, Vladimir, xiii, 3, 12-22, 23, 25, 29, 37, 38, 40, 57, 69, 103, 140, 174, 206, 207
  "The Americans Will Be Surprised," 21
  "Broadway," 13-14, 19-21, 68
  "Brooklyn Bridge," 18, 20, 103
  "A Challenge," 15
  "A Decent Citizen," 16-17
  "Farewell," 43
  "Homeward," 43
  "In a Loud Voice," 43
  "Mexico-New York," 19
  "My Discovery of America," 12-22
  "100%," 14-16
  "Poems about America," 12-22
Morozov, A., 167

Nazarenko, V., 55, 58, 63, 69
Negroes, 33, 39, 63-64, 83-84, 153-155

Nekrasov, Victor, xi, xii, 58, 64, 76, 79-116, 118, 119, 120, 126, 134, 136, 139, 141, 143, 150, 166, 202, 205
  First Acquaintance, 80, 88, 100, 105, 114
  In the Trenches of Stalingrad, 79
  Kira Georgievna, 80
  On Both Sides of the Ocean, 79-116
  Travels in Various Dimensions, 81
Nilsson, Nils Åke, 43

Pasternak, Boris, 59
Petrov, Evgeny, 117 (see Ilf)
Picasso, Pablo, 76, 77, 134
Pilnyak, Boris, xiii, 3, 23-30, 34, 38, 40, 206
  Okay, An American Novel, 23-30
  "Mahogany," 23-24
  The Naked Year, 23, 24
  "Tadzhikian Sketches," 24
  "The Unextinguished Moon," 23
Poe, Edgar Allan, "Ulalume," 144-145, 164, 165, 170-171
Pravda, xiii, 40, 198
Pushkin, Alexander S., "The Prophet," 144-145, 148, 162, 163, 169-170
Pyatnitsky, K. P., 11

Reavey, George, 43, 77
Reed, Mayne, 90, 91
Rodičev, N., 77
Rzhevsky, Leonid D., v, xi, 204

Sinyavsky, Andrei, 203
Skobelev, Eduard, 166
Sokolov, Mikhail, 183
Solzhenitsyn, Alexander, 3, 72, 80, 81

Steinbeck, John, 184
Stravinsky, Igor, 144-145

Tertz, Abram, 207-208
Todd, Albert C., 203-204
Tsvetaeva, Marina, 51, 76-77
Twain, Mark, ix, 6

Updike, John, 203-204

Voznesensky, Andrei, xi, xii, 42,
  49-78, 79, 80, 82, 84, 94,
  108, 113, 114, 119, 123, 140,
  150, 163, 165, 166, 173, 190,
  202, 205-207
  Antimiry, 65-67
  "The Artist," 52
  "Digression for Voice and
    Drums—Negroes Sing," 63-
    64
  "Digressions in the Form of
    Beatniks' Monologues," 61-
    63
  "Digression in the Rhythm
    of Rock 'n Roll," 60-61
  "Introductory," 52-54
  "June—1968," 74
  "The Master," 52
  "Monologue of Marilyn Mon-
    roe," 65-67, 192
  "Monologue with Footnotes,"
    68-71, 190
  "A New York Bird," 58-60,
    137
  "New York Buttons," 73-74
  "New York Night Airport,"
    56-58, 137
  "An Obligatory Digression,"
    64
  "OZA," 62-63
  "Striptease on Strike," 71-72
  Triangular Pear, 50-64, 76-77
  "Walkie-Talkie," 68, 71
  "Yet Another Introductory,"
    55-56, 59

Yevtushenko, Yevgeny, xi, xii,
  49, 58, 60, 72, 76, 120, 156,
  166, 168, 173-204, 205-206
  "The American Cemetery,"
    182
  "An American Nightingale,"
    177-179, 181, 201
  "Babii Yar," 198
  "A Ballad of Nuggets," 185-
    186
  "Ballad of Raised Fists," 198
  "A Boxer's Fate," 174-177
  "By the Forgotten Roman
    Way," 156, 197-198
  "Cemetery of Whales," 186-
    187, 198
  "Freedom to Kill," 198
  "Girl Beatnik," 179-181, 194
  "The Heirs of Stalin," 198
  "In a Steelworker's Home,"
    200-202
  "A Letter to John Steinbeck,"
    183-184
  "The Mark of Cain," 198
  "Monologue of a Broadway
    Actress," 191-192
  "Monologue of a Fox on an
    Alaskan Fur Farm," 188-
    189, 198
  "Monologue of an American
    Poet," 190-191
  "Monologue of an American
    Wanderer," 192-194
  "Monologue of a Teen-ager,"
    195-196, 198
  "Monologue of Doctor Spock,"
    198
  "Monologue of the Beatniks,"
    180-181
  "Poetry," 203
  "Slippery Ice in New York,"
    184
  "Smog," 194-195
  "Yes and No," 199